ROUTLEDGE LIBRARY EDITIONS:
BANKING & FINANCE

U.K. BANKING AFTER DEREGULATION

U.K. BANKING AFTER DEREGULATION

A. W. MULLINEUX

Volume 23

Routledge
Taylor & Francis Group
LONDON AND NEW YORK

First published in 1987

This edition first published in 2012
by Routledge
4 Park Square, Milton Park, Abingdon, Oxon OX14 4RN
605 Third Avenue, New York, NY 10017

Routledge is an imprint of the Taylor & Francis Group, an informa business

British Library Cataloguing in Publication Data
A catalogue record for this book is available from the British Library

ISBN: 978-0-415-52086-7 (Set)
ISBN: 978-0-203-10819-2 (ebk) (Set)
ISBN: 978-0-415-52672-2 (hbk) (Volume 23)
ISBN: 978-0-203-11684-5 (ebk) (Volume 23)

U.K. BANKING AFTER DEREGULATION

A.W. MULLINEUX

CROOM HELM
London • New York • Sydney

Croom Helm Ltd, Provident House, Burrell Row,
Beckenham, Kent, BR3 1AT
Croom Helm Australia, 44-50 Waterloo Road,
North Ryde, 2113, New South Wales

Published in the USA by
Croom Helm
in association with Methuen, Inc.
29 West 35th Street
New York, NY 10001

British Library Cataloguing in Publication Data

Mullineux, A.W.
U.K. banking after deregulation.
1. Banks and banking — Great Britain
2. Financial institutions — Law and
legislation — Great Britain
I. Title
332.1'0941 HG2988

ISBN 0-7099-4689-9

Library of Congress Cataloging-in-Publication Data

Mullineux, A.W.
U.K. banking after deregulation.

Bibliography: p.
Includes index.
1. Banks and banking — Great Britain. 2. Banks and banking — Great Britain — Deregulation. I. Title.
II. Title: UK banking after deregulation.
HG2988.M85 1987 332.1'0941 87-6742
ISBN 0-7099-4689-9

Printed and bound in Great Britain
by Billing & Sons Limited, Worcester.

To Judith

CONTENTS

PREFACE

This book had its origins in a course taught to students taking the Money Banking and Finance degree at the University of Birmingham (UK). The degree programme produced its first graduates in 1985. It covers only part of the course entitled 'Comparative Banking and Financial Systems', which undertakes a comparative study of banking systems and discusses various international and domestic financial issues. It is primarily concerned with the latter issues and is designed to serve as a textbook for students taking similar courses at other higher educational establishments. Given the topicality of the subject matter, it is hoped that it will also be of interest to people wishing to learn more about recent developments in the financial system.

I would like to thank my students, whose interest and comments have guided my writing. I would also like to thank Marylyn Mansell, for typing the various drafts of the book. Finally, I must thank Judith, for her encouragement.

University of Birmingham

PREFACE

This [illegible] [illegible] originally [illegible] taught to [illegible] [illegible] [illegible] [illegible] [illegible] [illegible] [illegible] [illegible] [illegible] [illegible] Religion and [illegible] System [illegible] [illegible] [illegible] [illegible] [illegible] [illegible] [illegible] [illegible]

[illegible] [illegible] it is hoped that it will [illegible] of interest [illegible] [illegible] [illegible]

[illegible] [illegible] [illegible] [illegible] [illegible] [illegible] [illegible]

[illegible]

Chapter One

DEREGULATION: AN INTERNATIONAL PERSPECTIVE

1.1 Introduction

At the outset it is worth stressing that the term deregulation, in the context of banking and financial systems, has adopted a wider meaning than its literal one. Historically, banking systems have been among the most heavily regulated sectors of most economies. This is because they have come to be regarded as unstable as a result of historical episodes such as the Great Crash in 1929 and the bank failures in the US in the 1930s. There is, however, a difference of opinion concerning the extent to which banking and financial systems are inherently unstable. Some economists (1) argue, for example, that periods of financial instability merely reflect underlying economic instability and that it is the economic, rather than the financial, system that is inherently unstable. The financial revolution that is spreading across the globe admittedly involves a sighificant amount of genuine deregulation or liberalisation, in the sense of the relaxation of restrictions, imposed by monetary authorities, on the provision of financial services and the freedom of movement of money and capital across national borders. The term deregulation has also come to be used to cover financial innovations (2), or what is sometimes called product deregulation. These innovations have been made possible by technological innovations in the financial sector, which have made use of rapidly advancing data processing capabilities and developments in international telecommunications systems. Incentives to introduce new financial instruments have come from the high inflation rates of the 1970s and the interest rate instability that resulted from the increased emphasis given by the monetary authorities of the major industrial countries, in the second half of the 1970s and the first half of the 1980s, to controlling the money supply as a means of reducing inflation. Another incentive has been the variability in exchange rates, following the introduction of floating exchange rates in the early 1970s (3), which in turn has added to interest rate instability because some countries have manipulated interest rates to influence their exchange rates, especially in times of crisis. The causes of financial innovation will be discussed further in Section 1.4

Financial innovation has led to an unbundling of services allowing banks to pursue more fee earning business in place of their traditional lending. Banks have progressed; from lending to placing first Eurobonds, then fixed rate Euronotes, then Floating Rate Notes (FRNs), and then offering Nifs, Rufs and Swaps (4) and ultimately to placing commercial paper. This process has become known as securitisation and it has led banks into closer involvement with the capital markets and allowed them effectively to make their loans tradable. It is a feature of the 1980s and was encouraged by the revised assessment of country risks following the 1982 Mexican debt crisis. Another contributory factor has been the growing sophistication of the treasury departments of their major, especially the multinational, corporate clients, which have sought instruments that will hedge against exchange and interest rate fluctuations. The process of securitisation has led to the development by banks of off balance sheet risks (5) because instruments such as Nifs involve contingent liabilities and they have thus explicitly or implicitly been underwriting these instruments. This has been of great concern to bank regulators (6) who have encouraged banks to provide capital backing for some of their off balance sheet risks, see Chapter 5. The rapidly developing US and Euro commercial paper markets, as well as the nascent (7) UK market, raise the possibility that major corporate clients may increasingly bypass the banking system altogether. The banks have so far managed to gain fee earning business by placing the paper (8) and by providing back up credit lines, which again involves them in off balance sheet risks.

These developments have led to a decline in the international syndicated loan market (9) and a merging of the capital and banking markets into a global pool. The banks have been losing their close relationships with corporate clients as competition has increased, between international financial institutions, for business. To retain corporate custom the major international banks have had to develop new financial instruments to match increasingly sophisticated corporate needs. Their international operations, developed significantly in the 1970s (10) have had to adopt an increasingly global perspective. Financial futures markets have been developed and the money and capital markets have become increasingly globalised, as twenty four hour trading, revolving around Tokyo, London and New York, has evolved. This first became a reality in the foreign exchange markets but latterly the capital markets have been considering the possibility of developing twenty four hour global trading in the shares of major companies.

There has thus been a certain amount of deregulation, in the sense of financial liberalisation, but there has also been a great deal of financial innovation involved in the financial revolution. The term deregulation will, in line with current usage, sometimes be used to cover both liberalisation and product deregulation, or innovation. Elsewhere it will be necessary to draw a distinction between deregulation and innovation. It should be stressed that there is a certain amount of re-regulation, or regulatory reform, going on. The regulatory apparatus for the financial system is receiving a major refurbishment in the UK for example, see Chapter 5. Also, as noted above, new regulatory requirements are being developed to cover off balance sheet risks. Deregulation does not therefore entail the abandonment of regulation and supervision of the financial system. It certainly makes supervision more difficult, by increasing the risk of incidence of fraud and bad practices, such as insider trading (11). The supervisors are, however, doing their best to keep abreast with developments by bolstering supervisory departments (12), increasing bad debt and capital requirements, and co-ordinating their efforts (13). The banking supervisors have made most progress towards co-ordination and exchange of information but the supervisors of the securities exchanges have also woken up to the need for increased co-operation (14). Given the merging of capital and banking markets these two groups of supervisors will also need to co-ordinate their efforts in the future and seem to be aware of this (15). They have the common objective of increasing the efficiency of the financial system whilst ensuring that crises do not occur which would force them to provide lender of last resort cover.

1.2 Deregulation of International Banking

White and Vittas (1986) review the deregulation, in the sense of the removal of long standing barriers to trade in financial services, in the international financial system that has occurred so far and assess future prospects for further deregulation. They note that the barriers being eroded include: those relating to domestic operations (16); restrictions on capital markets and exchange controls; and restrictions on foreign bank entry and the activities of foreign banks in domestic markets. Despite the various advances, the issue of restrictions on trade in services, financial or otherwise, has become a live one in international politics and has generated a great deal of wrangling in the preparation for the next round of multilateral Gatt negotiations. In September 1986 the participating nations agreed that the forthcoming Gatt negotiations would cover trade in services for the first time. Even within the European Community, restrictions on trade in, especially non-banking, financial services remain and the European Commission (1985) introduced proposals for further liberalisation.

The financial liberalisation that has so far occurred has not resulted from multilateral negotiations. There have been some bilateral negotiations, however. The most notable were those involving Japan and the US in 1983 and 1984. The US encouraged Japan to introduce deregulatory measures designed to promote the yen as an international currency in order to encourage a depreciation of the dollar with respect to the yen. There have also been negotiations involving British and Japanese monetary authorities concerning the access of financial institutions from one country to the other's financial markets (17). In general the deregulation has been prompted by concern about loss of business to less regulated, and especially offshore, centres and to the major financial centres, Tokyo, London and New York. But monetary authorities have also wished to encourage the development of more efficient financial systems.

Entry restrictions are the most visible examples of protectionism. Until the 1980s a number of major OECD (18) countries prohibited entry to domestic banking markets by foreign banks. Such controls have been removed in Norway (1985), Sweden (1985), Australia (1985), New Zealand (1985) and Canada (1980) and Japan, which granted securities licences, to a number of foreign investment and merchant banks and brokers, and trust banking licences, to nine foreign banks, in 1985. Blanket entry restrictions are now rare amongst industrialised countries, Iceland being the only OECD member country maintaining such restrictions. They are more prevalent amongst developing countries and, of course, remain intact in the Soviet bloc. Some industrialised countries continue, however, to restrict, formally or informally, the size of the foreign banking sector. Australia granted a total of 16 licences in 1985, for example, and Canada's foreign banking sector's assets are restricted to 16% of those of the domestic banking sector. There are proposals to remove the latter restriction. Elsewhere, in countries such as Italy, whose banking system is largely publicly owned, branching restrictions have inhibited foreign bank involvement. In 1985, however, Citibank (19) was permitted to buy into a small Italian bank. It thereby became the first foreign bank with a significant share in a branch network.

Once established, and often regardless of whether or not they are locally incorporated, which they are sometimes required to be, foreign banks still have restrictions imposed on the range of business they can undertake in some industrial countries. These too have been reduced. Germany allowed foreign banks to lead manage D.Mark Eurobond issues in 1985, for example, and Holland permitted foreign banks to lead manage Guilder Eurobond issues in 1986. Then in 1986 Germany invited foreign banks (20) to participate in the Federal Bond Consortium, which places government and other public sector bonds.

Additionally, foreign banks may face relatively strict regulatory requirements because they are often treated as self contained institutions in the enforcement of prudential liquidity and capital requirements by monetary authorities. They also have to comply with local regulations, which may be stricter than those in their country of origin. Canada, Japan and the US separate investment banking, which involves the provision of corporate advice, securities trading, underwriting and fund management, from commercial banking, which involves deposit taking and lending. The Japanese also separate investment banking from trust banking, which largely involves fund management. In contrast, Germany and Switzerland have long established universal banks which combine commercial and investment banking functions and banks in many European countries, most notably France and the UK, have been becoming more like universal banks since the 1970s. The restrictions in Japan, Canada and the US make entry into investment or commercial banking difficult for foreign banks which directly, or through subsidiaries, offer both investment and commercial banking services.

Such restrictions have raised the question of reciprocity, given that Japanese and US banks are permitted to engage in both investment and commercial banking, regardless of their domestic restrictions, in the UK and Germany for example. It was this that led to the negotiations between the UK and Japanese monetary authorities. Japanese securities houses were applying for UK banking licences which would have permitted them to undertake commercial banking business in the UK whilst UK banks were applying for securities licences in Japan. The Bank of England, in accordance with the Basle Concordat (21), wished to ensure that the investment banks were supervised by their domestic banking authorities. They were, however, regulated and supervised by the Ministry of Finance's Securities Division, rather than its Banking Division. Meanwhile UK banks and broking institutions were experiencing problems in their attempts to gain securities trading licences in Japan, the former because of the separation of investment and commercial banks there. An agreement was eventually reached between the monetary authorities of the two countries in 1986. UK commercial banks managed to gain entry by establishing subsidiaries that were part owned by non-banking companies (22). Reciprocity is currently actively pursued by Canada, the UK, Switzerland, Germany. In the UK a reciprocity clause was included in the Financial Services Bill, which is due to become law in 1987. During negotiations with the Japanese monetary authorities, the Department of Trade and Industry threatened to bring legislation on the relevant clause forward. Germany, meanwhile, has only invited foreign banks from countries offering reciprocal access to its own banks to lead manage D. Mark Eurobond issues and participate in the Federal Bond Consortium. Japanese banks have consequently not been invited to join the consortium.

The threat of losing business may eventually force convergence on Japan, Canada and the US. Japanese monetary officials have made statements encouraging further domestic liberalisation, and especially the removal of restrictions separating various types of banking business, which indicate that they are acutely aware of this possibility. The

Deputy Governor of the Bank of Japan, for example, has warned that the rapid expansion of the international business enjoyed by the Japanese institutions may in the future be inhibited by the proliferation of reciprocity clauses, and that business may be lost to offshore centres, unless further domestic deregulation is achieved. In particular the opposition from the various groups of domestic banks to the relaxation of the regulations separating them must be overcome and interest rate controls must be further liberalised. There has been a liberalisation of controls on interest rates paid on large short term and long term deposits but this should, he urged, be extended to smaller savings deposits - despite opposition from some banks and the post office saving system, which enjoys tax advantages and is very popular, and government officials, who want to protect the latter because it provides a useful stream of funds for the government. From a prudential point of view he argued that it was desirable to encourage the return of business lost to offshore centres, especially relating to the Euro-yen, in order to regulate it. Towards this end the authorities have also considered the promotion of Tokyo as an offshore financial centre. The US had experienced a similar loss of business offshore in the 1970s, as the Eurodollar markets grew apace, and was forced to respond by introducing International Banking Facilities (IBFs), see below, to win back some of the lost business. Reciprocity itself has given an impetus to more rapid liberalisation but it also carries the danger that in a period of retrenchment it might have the reverse effect.

Credit controls, on the growth of bank lending for example, can also discriminate against foreign banks. Restrictions on the growth permitted are naturally related to past reference points and this can hinder foreign banks which naturally start from relatively low lending positions. Credit controls are often combined with interest rate controls. Most of the industrialised countries have, after a period of encouraging the development of their money markets, moved away from credit controls towards a system of monetary control based on open market operations and allowed interest rates to become more responsive to market conditions. In 1985, for example, the French Socialist government replaced the Encaderment System with a more liberal regime of credit controls and in May 1986 the newly elected non-Socialist government promised to relax the remaining credit controls. Also in 1985 Sweden and

Norway freed banks from restrictions on lending and administered interest rates and so too did Italy, as part of an attempt to generate competition within the state controlled banking sector.

In France too access and competition between banks has been restricted by the level of state involvement. The big three banks have been nationalised since the war and there are other large state sponsored financial institutions. The Socialist government of the early 1980s nationalised most of the rest of the banking system in 1982. This followed a period in which the authorities had encouraged competition and diversification in the highly regulated banking system. It was felt at the end of the 1970s that rationalisation was urgently required. The Socialist government hoped to achieve this following nationalisation. The banking system was not, however, radically transformed and the current government proposes to denationalise the banking system, including the big three banks. Many developing countries, such as Mexico, also have state dominated banking systems which inhibit the opportunities for foreign banks.

As noted above, commercial banks have increasingly become involved in securities market business, first through the process of securitisation, especially in the Euromarkets, and latterly in the run up to the October 1986 Big Bang (23) in the UK. Many countries have become concerned about the potential loss of business to the three major financial centres, New York, London and Tokyo. The European countries are particularly worried about losing business to London after the Big Bang. Holland is determined to maintain and promote Amsterdam as a financial centre. Its capital markets were already relatively liberal but in 1985 and 1986 it has encouraged international linkages with foreign securities exchanges and further liberalisation. It does not wish to be left out of the developing market in globally traded securities. France too, under both the previous Socialist government and the present government, elected in March 1986, has introduced measures to promote share holding, liberalise the Paris Bourse, and improve the linkages between the regional bourses. Germany also has a fragmented capital market. It has tried to promote Frankfurt as a financial centre and to reduce the fragmentation by seeking an agreement between the eight regional bourses. The liberalisations have included a mixture of reforming trading practices, to bring them more in line with the New York and the London systems, reducing stamp duties, to encourage domestic shareholding and trading and provide depth to the markets, and reducing withholding and other taxes on interest and profit earned by foreign investors. Germany, for example, removed its withholding tax in 1985, following the initiative of the US, and plans to remove or reduce other levies and stamp duties. The Bundesbank also permitted the issue of D.Mark denominated Floating Rate Notes (FRNs), zero coupon bonds and currency swaps in 1985. The UK has also reduced its stamp duty significantly in the 1980s. The capital markets and trading practices in Tokyo remain inscrutable to foreigners but its importance as a financial centre is assured by the size of its domestic financial markets. It does, however, face competition in its time zone from S.E. Asian centres such as Hong Kong and Singapore. The prominence of New York is also supported by the size of its domestic economy. London's position is more precarious, because its economy is relatively small, hence the government's efforts to promote it as a major financial centre. In some of the industrialised economies, such as Spain, Italy and Greece, foreigners remain ineligible for stock exchange membership, however, and in France and Belgium only citizens of the EC can apply to join the stock exchange.

Fully competitive international banking and financial markets will be based on complete freedom of capital and money movements. This has been acknowledged by the European Commission, which has proposed (24) a programme for removing the remaining barriers to capital and money movements within the EC. Foreign exchange controls have been significantly reduced by industrial countries since 1979, when controls were removed in the UK. Many commentators believe that this initiative led inexorably to the Big Bang. In 1986 France and Italy removed some of their exchange controls, the previous Socialist government in France already having started the process of dismantling exchange controls in 1985. France has promised further liberalisation in the future. This deregulation may well give further impetus to financial liberalisation in those countries. Japan liberalised exchange controls in 1980 and, following the negotiations with the US Treasury in 1983/4, introduced further liberalisations with the purpose of encouraging the internationalisation of the yen and the development of a Euroyen market. In August 1986, for example, it increased the proportion of foreign assets that insurance and pension funds are permitted to hold in their portfolios, in an effort to encourage overseas investment and stem the appreciation of the yen, and in July 1986 it permitted trust banks to handle certain foreign currency trusts for the same reason. The US and Germany have long been free from exchange controls and restrictions on capital movements. Germany has, however, been wary of encouraging inward monetary flows, because the Bundesbank has been concerned about their effect on its ability to control the money supply and inflation. For this reason ECU accounts cannot be opened in Germany by its citizens, but ECU denominated bonds and other financial assets can be held. In May 1986, however, the Bundesbank did sanction the issue of D.Mark Certificates of Deposit (25), in a package of liberalising measures which also included the reduction of the minimum reserves that banks are required to hold at the Bundesbank. Cross border flows are also distorted by the variance in prudential reserve and reporting requirements, tax systems and banking secrecy laws, which make the Swiss financial centres relatively attractive for example. Until a more even treatment of financial institutions is achieved worldwide, such distortions will remain. The supervisors are actively co-ordinating their efforts and within the EC significant steps have been made towards harmonisation, but much work remains to be done. See White and Vittas (1986) for a discussion of the future prospects for the liberalisation of international banking and the means for promoting the removal of the remaining barriers.

Since the 1970s, the US has probably experienced more genuine financial deregulation than any other country. This is because, with the exception of Japan and possibly Canada, France and Italy, it had the most heavily regulated financial system of all the major industrial countries. It was markedly more heavily regulated than the German or Swiss systems, where universal banking has long been practised, for example. The UK has also enjoyed relative freedom from formal regulatory control. Until the 1979 Banking Act there was little formal banking legislation and supervision by the Bank of England has been relatively flexible and informal. Since the early 1970s traditional demarcations between the business undertaken by various classes of financial institutions have broken down. This is attributable to government prompted competition rather than formal deregulation, see Chapter 2. There have, however, subsequently been some more genuine deregulatory initiatives, such as the removal of exchange controls in 1979 and the measures discussed in Chapter 4, but there has also been a great deal of regulatory reform, see Chapter 5. In the next section the deregulation of the US banking system will be briefly reviewed.

1.3 **Deregulation in the US**

In the US, the Glass-Steagall Act (1933) prohibited interest payments on demand deposits and required interest rates on time and savings deposits to be limited. The infamous Regulation Q of the Federal Reserve Board (FRB) made this effective. Additionally, the Banking Act (1935) imposed limits on the interest rates paid by Federal Deposit Insurance Corporation (FDIC) insured banks, which are incorporated in its Regulation 29. The aim of this legislation was to protect the market position of 'thrifts', given their role in the provision of home loans and other consumer finance. The Hunt Commission Report (1971) advocated freer competition between banks and other deposit taking institutions. In the 1970s competition gradually developed and in the 1980s it has grown apace. A major event in the mid 1970s was the introduction by Savings and Loan Associations (SLAs) of NOW accounts (26), and other new financial instruments. These effectively allowed them to pay interest on current accounts. As a result of this seemingly unfair competition, banks were permitted to offer Automated Transfer System accounts from November 1978 and in January 1981 NOW accounts became legal throughout the banking system. The DIDMC Act (1980) (27) called for the abolition of all statutory interest rate ceilings over a 6 year period and permitted the general introduction of interest bearing cheque accounts. So far the effects of these changes have been to increase competition in the retail banking business, bidding up interest rates on retail deposits and down rates on loans and thereby cutting margins. The DIDMC Act set up a Depository Institution Deregulation Committee (DIDC) to oversee the phasing out of ceilings. In December 1982 the DIDC authorised Money Market Deposit Accounts (28) to be offered by all deposit taking institutions, free from interest rate restrictions; and from January 1983, it authorised super-NOW (29) accounts with unrestricted interest rates. The effects of these developments are illustrated by the fact that by the end of 1983 only 23% of deposits were non-interest bearing whilst in 1978 38% were.

These developments have altered the proportion of interest bearing assets in the targeted monetary aggregate and made monetary control more difficult. Hence the FRB's argument that it should not be expected to administer monetary policy unless it retains effective controls over the banking system to do so. The DIDMC Act (1980) gave the FRB broader authority to fix reserves and applies to all deposit taking institutions, rather than just the members of the Federal Reserve System (FRS). Previously only members of the FRS were subject to its reserve requirements and in return they received certain cheque clearing and payments services free. The opportunity cost of the non-interest bearing reserves deposited with the Federal Reserve Banks exceeded the benefits derived from these 'free' services and the member banks were, therefore, subject to an implicit tax. This was acting as a disincentive to FRS membership. The DIDMC Act reduced the reserves requirements on member banks and required the FRS to charge for its services in an effort to achieve a more efficient allocation of resources to payments services.

The DIDMC Act (1980) also permitted 'thrifts' (30) to offer services similar to commercial banks. This was reinforced by the Garn-St Germain Act (1982). These acts together not only allow 'thrifts' to offer a full range of retail banking services, but also to make commercial loans (31). The Garn-St Germain Act also aimed to revitalise the housing market by modifying regulations on 'thrifts' (32). In response to this increased competition in the retail sector, commercial banks have become more active in the mortgage market.

The Glass-Steagall Act (1933) also provided for the separation of securities business from banking by prohibiting banks from acting as agents in securities transactions, with brokers and dealers, and underwriting corporate securities. Similar legislation exists in Japan. In recent years, however, there has been a growing rivalry and competition between the banking and securities sectors. Banks have been offering brokerage services, securities firms have been offering cash management accounts, and the range of financial products and innovations has been expanding rapidly. Many US banks have found ways of offering insurance, discount brokerage, paper placement and a wide range of fee earning services to corporate clients. The banking laws specifically prevent banks from giving investment advice but they are able to act solely as agents and in offering discount broking services they attract business by charging low fees. They do not trade securities for their own accounts or underwrite them. Discount broking began on May 1st 1975, when the Securities and Exchange Commission (SEC) (33) eliminated fixed commissions in the New York Stock Exchange. Because of the Glass-Steagall Act, however, the impact of this deregulation was less than that expected in the UK following the October 1986 Big Bang (34). In November 1984 the chairman of the FDIC permitted smaller banks, which are non-members of the FRS, to enter the securities business. They were permitted to underwrite securities through separately capitalised subsidiaries. This was because of a loophole in the Glass-Steagall Act, which only applies to national banks and members of the FRS. It adds to the disincentive to join the FRS and presents a challenge to Congress to introduce new legislation.

The general increase in competition for deposits between 'thrifts', banks and securities houses has bid up interest rates. Banks are particularly fearful of competition, for their corporate business, from securities houses and have launched a counter offensive into the securities houses traditional business. In addition to their sortie into the discount broking business the banks have been active in the commercial paper (CP) market, which has grown rapidly in the 1980s. Debts outstanding in the market grew from just over $100bn in January 1980 to over $300bn in January 1986. The issuance of CP, which is short term negotiable debt sold directly by companies to investors in the money markets, allows corporate borrowers to bypass the banking system. The commercial banks have lost top class customers as the market has grown and been left with less creditworthy customers and problem loans to the troubled energy and farming sectors and to the Third World, especially the Latin American debtors. The banks have therefore been keen to earn fees from distributing CP to ensure that they do not lose touch with their major corporate clients. They view the distribution of CP as a natural extension of their banking business. The Securities and Investment Association (SIA), which is the trade association of investment banks and broking institutions, has contested the banks' right, in the light of the Glass-Steagall Act, to distribute CP and to provide discount broking services.

In January 1986 the Supreme Court ruled against the SIA and permitted commercial banks to offer discount broking services through subsidiaries. The case dated back to 1983, when the Comptroller (35) approved requests by banks to establish discount broking subsidiaries. In June 1986 County Bank, NatWest's merchant and investment banking subsidiary, became the first foreign bank to be permitted by the FRB to provide investment banking services. It was allowed to offer both broking and research facilities. Previously US law had been interpreted as preventing commercial banks, or their subsidiaries, from offering both services, confining them to one or the other. The ruling is likely to be contested by the SIA. County Bank was not permitted to underwrite securities, a business from which commercial banks and their subsidiaries remain excluded. In February 1986, however, a Federal Court ruled in favour of the SIA in its suit against Bankers Trust (BT), a major US commercial bank. BT had been permitted by the FRB to distribute CP because it did not judge the business to involve underwriting. The court ruled that the FRB had been wrong and that only Congress had the authority to permit banks to operate in the US commercial paper market. The court imposed a permanent injunction, preventing BT from selling CP on behalf of its clients because it judged the practice to contravene the Glass-Steagall Act. The commercial banks remain confident that the Supreme Court will eventually uphold the FRB's ruling. A decision in favour of the SIA could, however, tighten the Glass-Steagall Act and call into question deregulation that has so far proceeded through the favourable interpretation of legislation by banking supervisors. This would make new legislation all the more urgent. The US commercial banks expect to continue to be allowed to enter into investment banking business abroad, but may have to await legislation from Congress to permit similar developments in the US. The supervisors' position is conditioned by the worry that, if banks are not allowed to adapt to the short term needs of their corporate clients, they will lose their business and be forced to take a larger proportion of more risky business from less creditworthy customers. This contradicts the Glass-Steagall Act's purpose of reducing risks. Its origins lay in the financial crisis of the 1930s, which was attributed to banks' participation in more speculative investment banking business. It would be ironic if the Act ultimately had the effect of increasing commercial banking risks and causing another financial crisis.

The FRB is uneasy about banks moving into

discount broking and related business and is unlikely to encourage any further easing of the Glass-Steagall Act's provisions in the near future. The banks' expansion into discount broking has brought them under the supervisory purview of the SEC. It is not, however, a legal supervisor of banks in this business and legislation will be formally required to ensure banks are supervised in this area. The Reagan Administration favours regulation by function, which means that banks and other financial institutions entering new business should be subject to the existing regulations and overseen by the supervisory bodies in the new areas. The Justice Department has, however, ruled that the legal basis for the SEC to extend its jurisdiction to cover banks engaging in discount broking is 'unclear'. Competitive pressures are thus forcing banks to adopt new strategies and business and exposing them to new risks. Their regulators are urging caution, because the weak can undermine the strong in a period of transition. They argue that there is an urgent need to reform the banking laws, not necessarily to turn the clock back but to ensure that deregulation proceeds in a regulated and orderly manner. Some diversification is seen, by the FRB Chairman Paul Volcker, for example, as beneficial to the banking system in view of the encroachment on their traditional business by non-bank financial intermediaries. Caution is therefore urged and careful thought is being given to the permitted direction of diversification and the speed at which it should be allowed to occur.

The breakdown of the traditional demarcation of business in the financial services sector has raised the questions: what is money and what is a bank? Technological innovation in the financial sector, and particularly the development of electronic banking, could do away with cheques and perhaps eventually paper money. Money would then become guaranteed alpha-numeric data and a bank would be an institution that can provide both a guarantee and accounting services. Taking such a view telecommunications corporations and large retail stores might become the biggest threat to traditional commercial banks. Sears Roebuck for example has been rapidly developing the array of financial services it offers through its stores, and the trend is also evident in the UK (36). In September 1985, it introduced a nationwide credit card alongside its existing charge card in the US. It hopes that it will eventually rival Visa and Mastercard and link up the array of financial services it is offering, which include banking, insurance and brokerage services. There has been speculation in that market forces and technological innovation, which are pushing banks and non-bank financial intermediaries towards diversification, will eventually lead to hybrid financial intermediaries, which will effectively be broker-bankers, and to the development of financial supermarkets and conglomerates which may themselves be part of larger conglomerates. Given that this is a natural development regulators should not stand in the way but should develop a regulatory system capable of accommodating financial innovation. Banks in particular, because they are generally more heavily regulated, should be allowed to diversify to ensure uniformity of competition. As noted, Volcker and other regulators are not unsympathetic to the latter view but feel that deregulation should be regulated. The growth of financial and more broadly based conglomerates present their own problems for regulation and supervision as the JMB affair (37), in the UK, and the Banco Ambrosanio affair (38) amply illustrate. Also, many areas into which banks could diversify in the US are not uniformly regulated at the national level. The insurance industry, for example, is regulated at the state level. Under existing legislation a bank is defined by the Bank Holding Company (BHC) Act (1956) as an institution that both takes deposits and makes commercial loans.

The other major restriction on the banking industry in the US is that on branching. Both State and Federal Law include geographic restrictions. As a result, the US has approximately 14,000 commercial banks and 26,000 institutions offering some form of retail banking service and sometimes also services to the corporate sector. The McFadden Act (1927) and the Douglass Amendment to the Bank Holding Company (BHC) Act (1956) prohibit banks from offering banking services across state lines without permission from state authorities. Because of the definition of a bank it is, however, possible for banks to establish either deposit taking institutions, which make consumer loans and offer cheque accounts, or commercial loan making institutions across state lines, without contravening existing legislation. Banks have been exploiting this loophole in the early 1980s and establishing non-bank banks, which are more attractively called limited service banks. Most of these are effectively retail or consumer banks. US bank supervisors have consequently been swamped by applications from banks, non-bank financial intermediaries and other firms to establish limited service banks. The Office of the Comptroller of Currency (OCC) (39) declared them to be legal but introduced a temporary moratorium on applications and licensing in 1984, in the hope that the laws would be amended in legislation which was expected to be forthcoming from Congress. In the event no legislation was passed, the moratorium was lifted in October 1984, and the OCC began to process the 329 applications already filed by BHCs in their effort to proceed towards nationwide branching. The Garn-St Germain (1982) Act formally allowed banks to cross state lines to acquire failing institutions, although banks had been involved in assisted mergers organised by the FDIC for some time (40). De facto branching has been occurring for some time now, through the development of BHCs. Additionally national banks have been developing nationwide Automated Teller Machine (ATM) networks. If these are eventually permitted to take deposits and provide other services in addition to granting withdrawals then interstate banking could develop rapidly.

Recently groups of states have been making reciprocal agreements to allow branching and mergers across state lines. The New England banking experiment (41) is the broadest in scope and provides eventually for full interstate branching for banks indigenous to the participating states. The legality of such regional banking compacts, which exclude banks from other states and in particular the big money centre banks, was challenged by Citicorp. Following a protracted legal battle the Supreme Court upheld their legality in June 1985. It has been estimated that mergers involving banks within the regional state groupings could eventually lead to half a dozen regional banking groups with assets sufficient to rank them in the top 15 US banks. The money centre banks must meanwhile rely on developing limited service bank and ATM networks.

As a result of two rulings by the Department of Justice on bank mergers in 1981 the banking supervisors must find a trust law violation before they can prevent a merger that does not contravene federal or state laws. There is plenty of scope for consolidation in the banking industry before mergers imply concentration ratios sufficiently large to violate trust laws. This is especially true if 'thrifts' and perhaps other non-bank financial intermediaries are included in the industry, alongside banks. As a result, in May 1984 the FRB approved two interstate bank mergers, whereas in the past it had only permitted mergers involving troubled banks.

A bill has recently been tabled by the Congressional Banking Committee which will remove all interstate banking barriers, after five years, among states with reciprocal legislation. A regional merger wave is predicted in preparation for exposure to competition from the money centre banks and Ohio and Maryland have already permitted mergers.

Nationwide banking, therefore, seems inevitable and could develop rapidly once branching restrictions are fully lifted, since all the building blocks are already in place. The main problem for the regulators is to ensure that branching proceeds equitably and that the merger wave does not lead to overconcentration and reduced competition.

Another significant development has been the decision, by the FRB, to permit the establishment of International Banking Facilities (IBFs) in the USA since 1981. The IBFs are relatively free from regulation and enjoy tax concessions. They are supposed to allow American banks to compete more fairly with foreign banks which have branches in the USA. The objective is to attract some of the Eurodollar market business to the States and to re-indigenise some of the international banking business lost to offshore banking centres, especially those in the Caribbean. IBFs are not permitted to conduct business with local residents, they are supposed to be purely for international banking operations. Foreign banks are also allowed to establish IBFs and, consequently, the USA is, effectively, offering offshore banking facilities. Previously banks were able to establish branches almost anywhere in the USA, under the Edge Act (42), provided that they specialised in business abroad or the finance of foreign trade. The difference between the Edge Act companies and the IBFs is that the latter are relatively free from regulation and enjoy a more conducive taxation environment but cannot deal with US citizens; Edge Act companies can, but only in relation to international business.

Deregulation has thus led to de facto branching and the blurring of distinctions and increased competition between commercial and investment banks, 'thrifts', and non-bank financial intermediaries. In many cases this has proceeded through the exploitation of loopholes in existing legislation rather than through formal amendments to regulations. It is probably impossible to return to the position envisaged by existing legislation but new legislation is being requested by the supervisors to ensure that any future deregulation proceeds in a controlled manner, so that the additional risks being undertaken by financial institutions moving into new fields can be monitored and, where necessary, contained or at least provisioned for.

1.4 **Causes of Deregulation**

Deregulation has two strands, liberalisation and financial innovation. To some extent they have separate causes although they are interrelated. Liberalisation has proceeded internationally as well as domestically. The main spur to opening access to foreign financial institutions, for many countries, has been to attempt to promote their financial centres in the face of globalisation which threatens increasingly to revolve around London, New York and Tokyo. The opening up of financial systems to foreign competition, however, brings its own pressures for domestic liberalisation, to achieve conformity with practices elsewhere. A process of competitve liberalisation seems to have developed. Germany has had one of the most liberalised banking systems, amongst the major industrial nations, during the post war period. In the UK and France, banking systems have, since the 1970s, moved towards the German universal banking system as traditional demarcations between financial institutions have been eroded. Following the Great Depression, largely as a result of the Glass-Steagall Act, the US has three distinct groups of financial institutions: investment banks; 'thrifts' and commercial banks; and insurance companies. In the latter half of the 1970s, the investment banks introduced Money Management Deposit Accounts (MMDAs) with transactions facilities; life insurance companies developed links with investment banks; 'thrifts' introduced NOW accounts and began to compete more directly with commercial banks; banks moved into the securities and insurance markets; and retailing companies, such as Sears Roebuck, began to sell financial services. The US deregulation in the early 1980s can be seen as a response to this build up of pressure for change and an attempt to catch up with developments abroad.

Domestic liberalisation introduces banks and other financial institutions to new markets, increases competition and reduces margins, and provides an environment in which profits can be made by offering new products, perhaps developed as a result of experiences in other markets. Technology is often seen as a driving force to financial innovation. Although obviously invaluable in developing new products and international linkages it is unlikely to have done more than facilitate change. Most of the technology was, after all, already available before its potential was realised by financial institutions.

For opportunities to be exploited the demand for the products must exist. Here too domestic financial developments have had an impact. The increasing dominance of stock markets by pension and insurance companies, especially in the UK (43) and the US, has, for example, led fund managers increasingly to want to deal with banks and broking firms as principals. They have wished to buy and sell shares and bonds in large blocks. Private shareholders have insufficient capital to trade in blocks and so the financial intermediaries have increasingly used their capital to trade on their own account. In so doing they incur market risks previously borne by their customers. They have consequently developed complex hedging techniques to reduce the risks they face as principals. The other driving forces, creating a demand among customers for new financial instruments, have been high inflation and volatile interest and exchange rates.

In the US for example, monetary control concentrated in the 1970s on the retail banking market, which was separated from the wholesale banking market. When inflation accelerated in the latter half of the 1970s interest rates on the wholesale markets began to rise but they were constrained from doing so in the retail sector due to Regulation Q and related interest rate restrictions. A differential consequently grew between retail and wholesale rates and the gap was filled by Money Market Mutual Funds (MMMFs). These were effectively unit trusts which collected deposits, invested them in marketable securities, and paid their customers interest at money market levels net of costs. The household sector transferred funds from savings accounts and cashed in insurance policies to invest in MMMFs. This development forced the loosening of controls on banks and 'thrifts', and banks were permitted to open MM accounts. By the mid 1980s 90% of savings accounts bore market related interest and 40% of current accounts bore interest. Another consequence was the erosion of the segmentation between the unregulated wholesale and the regulated retail sectors. Finally it led to the erosion of the barriers erected to separate investment and commercial banking and insurance.

In the UK the gap between the retail and wholesale rates was less pronounced and it took longer to stimulate change. Since the early 1980s, however, merchant banks and building societies have been offering market related interest bearing cheque accounts and the clearing banks have followed suit. In the UK financial diversification continues to proceed rapidly but opinion concerning its merits is more divided in the US, where Congressional legislation relating to branching and the separation of investment and commercial banking is still awaited. Interest and exchange rate volatility has also been a major causal factor in financial innovation. It has primarily encouraged the development of hedging devices such as interest rate and foreign currency swaps and the futures markets.

If inflation was perhaps the major driving force then the question must be asked whether the fall in inflation will bring financial innovation to an end and perhaps even cause a reversion to more traditional instruments. Similarly, to the extent that exchange rate stability is increased following the Plaza accord (44) and this, combined with the fall in inflation, allows lower and more stable interest rates, the need for hedging devices may decline. The deregulation achieved so far has increased competition which provides its own spur to continued financial innovation in order to seek out and meet the needs of retail and corporate customers. Financial institutions have in the 1980s become acutely aware of the possibility of cross-selling financial products once they have opened up contacts with clients. They, therefore, have an incentive to continue to diversify. Thus even if financial innovation declines in pace, the breakdown of barriers between financial institutions is likely to continue and financial supermarkets, offering a whole range of financial services at one location, are likely to develop, at least in the UK and Europe. There may of course still be room for specialist financial institutions and financial boutiques, as there are in other retail businesses.

In the US prospects are less clear. Branching restrictions and the Glass-Steagall Act still inhibit such developments. This continues to put their commercial banks at a disadvantage compared to non-financial firms, especially those in the retail sector such as Sears Roebuck and Penny's, which already have a good geographical distribution. The commercial banks have also suffered from competition from investment banks with well developed distribution systems, such as Meryll Lynch, which can cross sell other financial services. Whilst the restrictions remain in place, however, the US financial system is likely to continue to lead the way in financial innovation, in order to circumvent them. Similarly the banks are likely to continue to develop joint ventures with other banks and financial institutions to allow them to achieve effective nationwide branching and earn fees from the cross selling of financial services.

1.5 Future Developments and Consequences

Deregulation, which has accelerated in the 1980s, is transforming banking systems in various countries. Merchant and clearing banks in the UK are actively developing investment banking divisions and subsidiaries. The major clearing banks are metamorphosing into universal banks. The convergence of the international banking and capital markets is creating a global pool of funds and forcing major international banks to transform themselves from intermediaries between depositors and borrowers into financial engineers trying to match the requirements of investors and capital users. Their traditional relationships with corporate clients have been breaking down as competition to meet the needs of corporate, and government, clients, who have demanded increased flexibility, has increased. In their non-retail banking business, banks are becoming deal makers rather than loan makers.

The process of securitisation has been encouraged by the fall in inflation in the mid 1980s. Large creditworthy borrowers have enjoyed access to cheaper funds whilst lenders have enjoyed substantial capital gains as interest rates have fallen with inflation. Opportunities for realising capital gains have added to the liquidity of the markets, making securities more readily tradable. This virtuous circle could easily be broken if inflation were to start to rise again. The contingent liabilities that have resulted from the development of off balance sheet business could be called upon and the insurance companies that have begun to underwrite banking risks would also be exposed. It is to be hoped that the central banks and the regulators overseeing the securities and insurance businesses can agree on an allocation of lender of last resort responsibilities long before the threat of a crisis arises. If a crisis did occur it would bring in its wake calls for re-regulation. By then the major international financial institutions may well have grown to the point of being virtually uncontrollable by the regulatory authorities in their country of origin. The continued development of co-ordinated supervision, therefore, appears essential. Alternatively, consideration could be given to the development of a supra-national authority, perhaps by enhancing the powers of the IMF.

The chances of re-regulation are probably highest in the US. If the fall in the dollar were to discourage Japanese investment in US Treasury Bonds and the US budget deficit proved difficult to reduce in the ensuing period of reduced and perhaps declining or negative US growth, then the problem of funding the deficit would assume massive proportions. The US would then find it increasingly difficult to service its trade deficit and its accumulating foreign debts. Drastic financial reform, to encourage domestic savings and channel them into the government's coffers, might be required and exchange controls might even be introduced.

More generally, the compatibility of free capital movement and free trade may have to be re-evaluated. The growing freedom in capital flows has gone hand in hand with growing protectionism. If this is a causal relationship, then the perspicacity of sacrificing free trade in goods and non-financial services for financial freedom may be questioned. It may, however, be that the problem lies in the incompatibility of floating exchange rates and free capital flows and that reform of the international monetary system is required. The introduction of exchange rate target zones, for the major international reserve currencies, and improved international policy co-ordination might well reduce the volume of capital flows and prevent the sustained currency misalignments which have been the main cause of trade imbalances. If this prognosis is incorrect, or if the international monetary system is not reformed along these lines, then, possibly after a damaging trade war, pressures to restrict the freedom of capital flows might re-emerge. At present freer capital movements are increasing international economic interdependence and restricting the economic policy options open to governments, forcing them to adopt policies akin to the deflationary ones pursued by the majority of the leading industrial countries. It may indeed have been the deflationary policies, rather than free capital flows *per se*, that have generated the resurgence in protectionism. The French Socialist government of the early 1980s, for example, had, due to pressure on the franc, to abandon its Keynesian growth oriented policies for monetary and budgetary discipline. Pressure for re-regulation and control of capital flows may, therefore, come following a coincident return of governments with a more Keynesian outlook in the major industrial countries. A future UK Labour government might be expected to support an international move to reintroduce exchange controls for example.

Deregulation so far seems to have increased risks in the banking system. The developing commercial paper markets are leading major corporate borrowers to bypass the banking system and leaving banks with more risky assets. Governments seem to be competing, on behalf of their financial systems, for international securities business by lowering regulatory standards. The lack of understanding, professed by supervisors, practitioners and clients, about the increasingly complex new financial instruments being developed is a major cause for concern. The supervisors (45) have expressed concern about the lack of detailed information and feel unable to assess risks adequately. They fear that the instruments are being priced too finely because inadequate risk premiums are being charged. There is a general concern that speculative movements of capital are based on globally available disinformation as well as information. To the extent that this is true, speculative movements are more likely to be destabilising than stabilising. In the retail banking sector concern is growing (46) that competition for loan business is encouraging consumers to build up levels of debt that they will not be able to manage if interest rates rise appreciably. This is a further factor reducing the quality of bank assets. Additionally, the legal basis of the new instruments has been by no means fully tested. Contractual obligations could be contested when the pressure is on. More generally, financial institutions are moving into new business. Banks are becoming more like non-bank financial intermediaries and vice versa. They may not appreciate fully the risks involved in their new businesses. Developments in office banking may encourage a further breakdown in the associations between banks and their individual customers (47). Consumers of retail banking services have already proved willing to shop around for loans and money transmission services and the development of home banking (48) might well further distance banks from their retail customers.

The tendency for consumers of banking services to deal with numerous financial institutions makes it difficult for the banks to assess the financial position of their customers and introduces additional risks. Further, the development of electronic banking, which makes money transfers more easy and rapid, is likely to continue to increase the flows of hot money domestically and internationally. This may make domestic monetary control virtually impossible (49). If these monetary flows cause instability in the inflation rate, then governments may in the future move to restrict them by introducing re-regulatory measures.

In the light of the growing risks many commentators believe that the next step will be consolidation. This would allow stronger institutions to absorb their weaker brethren and to develop large diversified portfolios, enabling them to pool and spread the risks and make larger profits, which also afford protection against unforeseen contingencies. The larger European banks are becoming conglomerates and already moving in this direction. The US and Japanese banks are also doing this internationally but face restrictions on such developments in their domestic markets. Rybcynski (1985) has argued that consolidation, diversification and conglomeration will increase a financial system's and, therefore, an economy's ability to assume risk. Such developments are, therefore, a good thing and may be the natural course in the current economic environment. It is worth noting that the trend in the non-financial services and manufacturing sectors has been away from conglomerates. The 1970s and early 1980s have witnessed an increasing number of divestments and management buyouts. For the financial conglomerates to be successful there must be an efficient management structure. It is by no means obvious that this will be less difficult to deliver in the financial sector than it proved in the non-financial sector. The opportunities for economies of scale, risk management and managerial control, offered through technological innovation, might, however, ensure that financial conglomerates will be efficient. The mergers and acquisitions wave experienced in the corporate sectors of the US and other countries in the first half of the 1980s may anyway indicate a shift back in favour of conglomerates.

If the financial system is inherently unstable we may find out in the not too distant future. Economic prospects in the mid 1980s were not very rosy, however, and should a crisis occur it might prove difficult to disentangle the causes. It seems likely that world economic prospects, freedom of trade, and stable foreign exchange markets and financial systems are interrelated, as seemed to be realised, following the interwar depression, in the postwar period. It would be a tragedy for the world to have to go through another depression to drive this message home but this is the risk we face unless speculative capital flows can be abated. The flows could either be restricted, by re-regulation, or reduced, through increased international economic co-operation leading to a co-ordinated economic expansion and a reformed international monetary system. Whichever solution is chosen, it seems clear that economic prospects should not be sacrificed in the name of financial freedom, which is after all supposed to generate financial efficiency with the aim of improving economic performance.

1.6 <u>The Rest of the Book</u>

Having, in this chapter, provided an international perspective on financial deregulation, the rest of the book concentrates on financial deregulation in the UK and is organised as follows. Chapter 2 concentrates on the reform of the UK banking and clearing system, which has been driven by increased competition encouraged by the monetary authorities. Chapter 3 outlines the development of electronic banking in the UK, which has been caused by the increasing cost of paper funds transfer and by technological innovation and conditioned by government encouraged competition. Chapter 4 considers wider deregulatory pressures resulting from: government legislation concerning the Building Societies and the Trustee Savings Banks; and the government's decisions to remove exchange controls in 1979 and to strike a deal with the Stock Exchange, in 1983, concerning the ending of fixed commissions and other restrictive practices relating to membership. Chapter 5 relates the UK monetary authorities' regulatory and supervisory responses to the deregulatory developments, and notes their relationship to international banking supervisory initiatives. The final chapter speculates briefly about the implications of the financial revolution for the financial system of the future and assesses prospective developments in the UK banking and financial system in the more immediate future.

Notes

1. See Niehans (1978, Chapter 12) for further discussion.

2. See Bank for International Settlements (1986) for a discussion of recent financial innovations.

3. Following the breakdown of the Smithsonian Agreement, see for example Grubel (1984) for details.

4. See Bank for International Settlements (1986) for details.

5. I.e. risks related to activities that cannot be regarded as assets or liabilities and do not, therefore, show up on the balance sheet.

6. See Committee on Banking Regulations and Supervisory Practices (1986).

7. See Chapter 4 for further discussion.

8. See Section 1.2.

9. Which had grown following the rise in oil prices instigated by the Organisation of Petroleum Exporting Countries (OPEC) in 1973 as a means of recycling the resultant OPEC surpluses. The biggest recipients of the loans were developing countries, the largest being the major Latin American countries. The Mexican Crisis, see Kraft (1984), discouraged further growth in the market.

10. Due to the OPEC surplus recycling.

11. Which involves trading on an institution's own account using confidential information to which an advisory, or some other, department is supposedly privy.

12. In 1986 the Bank of England, for example, expanded its supervisory division significantly.

13. Through the Committee on Banking Regulations and Supervisory Practices which meets at the Bank for International Settlements in Basle.

14. At the annual meeting of the International Association of Securities Associations in July 1986 in Paris, a fundamental reform of the organisation was agreed with the aim of turning it into a genuine international securities watchdog.

15. See Governor's Speech, Bank of England (1986a).

16. See Germany and Morton (1985) for a survey of financial deregulation in advanced countries.

17. These commenced in 1985 and an agreement was reached in 1986, see below.

18. Organisation for Economic Co-operation and Development.

19. The banking subsidiary of the US's largest financial conglomerate, Citicorp.

20. From countries allowing German banks similar access to their own government bond markets, see below on reciprocity.

21. See Committee on Banking Regulations and Supervisory Practices (1975 and 1983).

22. A means of entry first discovered by Deutschebank of Germany. Barclays announced plans to follow a similar route

in May 1985. It has had a commercial banking branch in Japan since 1972 and in May 1986 it became one of nine foreign banks permitted to open a trust banking subsidiary, which will seek to attract fund management business, in Tokyo.

23. The reform of the UK Stock Exchange, see Chapter 4.

24. See European Commission (1986).

25. Which give evidence of deposits made with a bank and are repayable on a fixed date. Depositors can hold the certificates until maturity or sell them.

26. Negotiable Order of Withdrawal, see Simpson and Parkinson (1984).

27. Depository Institutions Deregulation and Monetary Control Act.

28. See Simpson and Parkinson (1984).

29. See Simpson and Parkinson (1984).

30. Savings and loan associations, savings banks and credit unions.

31. See Heaton and Dunham (1985).

32. By increasing their lending limits, for example.

33. The SEC has statutory powers to regulate the US securities market.

34. See Chapter 4.

35. See note 39.

36. See Chapter 3.

37. Johnson Matthey Bank was part of a largely non-financial conglomerate and had to be bailed out by the Bank of England, with the help of a group of banks and bullion dealers, in October 1984.

38. Banco Ambrosanio's Luxembourg subsidiary was a holding company and when it got into trouble, in 1982, the Luxembourg and Italian monetary authorities both disclaimed supervisory responsibility, exposing a loophole in the 1975 Basle Concordat, see Chapter 5, and refused to extend lender of last resort cover because of its non-bank status.

39. Which is a department of the Treasury headed by the Comptroller of Currency and shares supervisory authority with the FRB, the FDIC and the state authorities.

40. The FDIC has called for further legislation to speed up acquisitions of failing banks.

41. See Syron (1984) and Dunham and Syron (1984).

42. Which was an amendment, passed in 1919, to the Federal Reserve Act initiated by Senator Walter Edge.

43. In the UK the Thatcher government has tried to reverse this trend in the 1980s, through its privatisation programme and a series of measures designed to encourage wider share ownership. Initial estimates of the short term impact of this policy have varied considerably and because the shares may ultimately be sold by private holders, and purchased by financial institutions, it may be some time before the success of the policy can be accurately gauged.

44. An agreement, between the Group of 5 finance

ministers and their deputies, to undertake co-ordinated intervention to bring down the value of the dollar, reached at the Plaza Hotel, New York, in September 1985.

45. See Committee on Banking Regulations and Supervisory Practices (1986).

46. In May 1986, for example, the Chairman of the Building Societies Association urged its members to guard against encouraging people to borrow more than they could afford and in August 1986 the Chairman of Barclays, presenting the bank's half yearly report, advised both lenders and borrowers to show restraint. The National Consumer Council's working party on consumers and debt has also expressed its increasing concern about the problems created by competition to lend money, especially in the home loans market.

47. Office banking involves the plugging into banking services through office terminals. Hitherto these have been supplied by the particular bank with which the company does business. In the future it is likely that offices will have access to financial services at a number of institutions through standardised terminals.

48. Home banking is less developed than office banking, probably because of the relative costs of supplying terminals to households vis-à-vis businesses. The experiments undertaken in the UK by the Royal Bank of Scotland and the Nottingham Building Society tie the consumer to the services of particular institutions. As with office banking, future developments may give consumers access to the services of a number of competing institutions.

49. See Bank for International Settlements (1986) and Niehans (1983).

Chapter Two

REFORMING THE BRITISH CLEARING BANKS

2.1 The Ending of the Interest Rate Cartel and Subsequent Developments

The development of the UK banking system since 1971 has been influenced significantly by changes in methods of monetary control.

There have been two major policy announcements, concerning monetary control, in recent history: "Competition and Credit Control" (1) (CCC) in 1971; and "Monetary Control Provisions" (2) in 1981. These announcements involved major changes in the scope and operation of monetary and credit controls.

Prior to 1971, the rate of interest (Bank Rate (3)) was controlled using open market operations (omos) and, additionally, both quantitative guidance, in the form of credit growth ceilings, and qualitative guidance, to direct lending towards investment and exports for example, were used to control credit flows. Cash and liquidity ratios were imposed on the clearing banks, as levers on which omos could operate. These ratios had been changed from time to time but, immediately prior to the introduction of CCC, the liquidity ratio was 28% and was rendered variable by calls for interest bearing, special deposits (4).

The fundamental aim of CCC was to control credit creation using interest rate variations brought about by omos; that is, by manipulating the price of credit. Quantitative and qualitative guidance was dropped, with the proviso that it would be reintroduced if needed. The liquidity and cash ratios were replaced by a Reserve Asset Ratio (RAR) and the eligible reserve assets were redefined. The RAR was to be rendered variable by calls for interest bearing, special deposits. The clearing banks, and some of the other financial institutions under the supervisory wing of the Bank of England, were required to hold a 12½% ratio of reserve assets to eligible liabilities (5). The previous cash and liquidity ratios had applied only to the clearing banks. Under the CCC arrangements, finance houses, for example, were required to adhere to RARs. The clearing banks, however, remained the only institutions that were required to hold cash deposits with the Bank of England. These cash deposits were set at 1½% of their eligible liabilities. They qualified as reserve assets, but no interest was required to be paid on them. Their purposes were: to satisfy interbank clearing needs and to provide the Bank of England with an adequate source of revenue. The clearing banks argued that they were an unfair imposition on them (6) because they should only be required to hold cash deposits with the Bank of England sufficient for clearing purposes. They felt that the responsibility for the provision of funds to the Bank should have been evenly spread throughout the banking system.

The choice of eligible reserve assets ensured a role for the discount market. Members of the London Discount Market Association (LDMA) agreed to purchase all the treasury bills offered at the weekly tender. Between 1971 and 1981, the Bank of England commonly offered more treasury bills than were required to finance the government's day to day operations, with the intention of creating shortages of cash in the money markets. The cash balances at the Bank of England became the fulcrum of the system of monetary control (7). Treasury bill sales resulted in commercial bank balances at the Bank of England being run down. This in turn forced banks to withdraw 'money at call' from the discount market. The discount houses then became short of cash and had to turn to the Bank, as 'lender of last resort', for funds. These funds could be supplied at a rate of interest largely of the Bank's own choosing. Hence the Bank of England could attempt to control the rate of interest through omos.

In October 1972 the Minimum Lending Rate (MLR) was introduced. This differed from the Bank Rate, the rate set by the Bank of England at which it was willing to lend to the discount houses, in that it was calculated by a formula related to market interest rates. The formula was abandoned from time to time, to allow the Bank more discretion.

The 'competition' part of CCC provided for the abandonment of the interest rate cartel operated by the Committee of London Clearing Banks. The major clearing banks were encouraged to set lending and borrowing rates competitively. The abandonment of the interest rate cartel had been advocated in reports by the National Board for Prices and Incomes and by the Monopolies Commission (8), in connection with its investigation of the proposed merger between Barclays, Lloyds and Martins banks. The ending of the cartel had the effect of allowing the clearing banks to compete for funds effectively and directly, rather than indirectly through subsidiaries, in the interbank market. CCC did not cover all deposit taking institutions. In particular, the secondary or fringe banks were not covered (9).

By the end of 1973 it became evident that lending was not under control, despite record interest rate levels. Still higher rates were regarded as politically unacceptable and potentially damaging to the economy. Hence the Supplementary Special Deposit Scheme (SSDS) or 'corset' was introduced. Under the SSDS, the clearing banks were required to lodge Supplementary Special Deposits (SSDs) with the Bank of England when the growth of their interest bearing eligible liabilities exceeded a predetermined guideline and were punished by not receiving interest on the SSDs.

The introduction of the SSDS was a major break with the principles of CCC because it marked the return to directly administered control over bank lending. The 'corset' was finally abandoned in June 1980, following the budget. After 1971, the Bank continued to give qualitative lending directives to the clearing banks and additionally, in the 1971-1981 period, there were restrictions in force concerning finance house operations and consumer loans. Minimum downpayments or contributions were commonly required for purchase of consumer durables and houses, and restrictions were imposed on periods of repayment. These term, and other, controls on consumer credit were lifted in July 1982.

A major problem with the 'corset' was that it caused 'disintermediation'. Lending normally made by the clearing banks, and consequently registered in sterling M3 growth, was diverted through other, uncontrolled, institutions and markets. A major source of disintermediation was 'bill-leak'. Banks directly or indirectly, through subsidiaries, accepted commercial bills, issued by companies, who then sold them to the public to raise funds. The use of commercial bills for borrowing increased rapidly during the periods in which the 'corset' was in operation (10). The size of the disintermediation was emphasised by the severe distortion, in 1980/81 and to some extent in 1981/82, of sterling M3 growth following the final removal of the 'corset' in June 1980. This distortion was caused by reintermediation, as direct bank lending increased and 'bill-leak' declined. Given that the 'corset' had outlived its usefulness and created severe distortions within the financial system, an alternative method of monetary control was clearly required.

In March 1980 a Green Paper (11), which aimed to stimulate discussion about methods of monetary control, was published. It discussed in detail the operation of monetary control in the post CCC period and considered a number of alternative methods of monetary control. It concluded: that the 'corset' should be lifted; that the RAR was superfluous as a means of interest or credit control; that a cash requirement was a necessary fulcrum of monetary policy, but that the 1½% ratio imposed on the London clearing banks should be replaced by a ratio applying to all banks; and that special deposits should be retained as a policy instrument.

The paper discussed two alternative approaches to monetary control: a monetary base indicator system; and a monetary base control system. The monetary base indicator system would require banks to maintain a ratio of base money to liabilities and the authorities would use deviations from it as an indicator of the need to change short term interest rates. The monetary base control system would involve manipulating the supply of base money with the purpose of controlling the money supply, as measured by some monetary aggregate. Problems such as the definition of the set of assets to be included in the monetary base, the appropriate monetary aggregate to act as an intermediate target, and whether the base ratios were to be mandatory or voluntarily arrived at, were left unresolved.

Following consultation, with the banks and other interested parties, a new system of monetary control was announced in August 1981. It was described in a document entitled: "Monetary Control Provisions" (12). These provisions covered a newly defined monetary sector, which was wider than the banking sector previously considered in the pursuit of monetary policy and included licensed deposit taking institutions (LDTs) (13). The MLR was put on ice, in order to allow the markets to play a greater role in the determination of interest rates. It has since made only one reappearance, in the January 1985 sterling crisis, when the Bank wanted to raise interest rates rapidly.

Other major changes were also made. The Bank ceased to quote the price at which the members of the LDMA could sell Treasury bills to the Bank of England. The discount houses were instead required to set their own prices and the Bank could decline to buy the bills if the price was not in accordance with its wishes. The list of acceptable, to the Bank, bills was redefined to ensure a sufficient supply of bills. This was achieved by extending the list of banks eligible to accept bills. The position of the discount houses, as market makers in these bills, was assured by requiring eligible banks to maintain, on average, 6% of their eligible liabilities as money at call with the LDMA, subject to these deposits not falling below 4% of eligible liabilities on any one day. This became known as 'club money' and the requirement was subsequently revised so that the average deposit became 5% of their assets and the minimum 2½%. The RAR was abolished and so was the requirement that the London clearing banks hold 1½% of their eligible liabilities as non-interest bearing cash deposits with the Bank of England. Instead, all institutions with liabilities in excess of £10m were required to keep ½% of their eligible liabilities as non-interest bearing cash deposits with the Bank of England. This was designed to provide the bank with a sufficient source of income. The London clearing banks were encouraged to maintain larger cash deposits in accordance with their interbank clearing needs. Special deposits, on which interest would be paid, could still be called.

The monetary control mechanism was thus broadly unchanged from that underlying CCC. Omos were still supposed to be the main instrument and they were to be conducted through the discount market. The aim was still to manipulate the short term interest rate in an effort to control the growth of the money supply. Interest rates were, however, supposed to be more flexible and market influenced, following the abandonment of the MLR. The banks were thus less vulnerable to 'round tripping' (14) and related prudential risks. The 1981 "Provisions" also introduced a framework within which a non-mandatory system of base control could be operated. Once the clearing banks had determined their equilibrium voluntary balances at the Bank of England, for clearing purposes, then the Bank could attempt to manipulate the monetary base by operating on these balances, through omos.

Monetary control, after 1981, was not in fact entirely effected through short term omos in Treasury and commercial bills. Instead, the monetary authorities resorted to 'overfunding', which involved the sale of more bonds than were necessary to finance the Public Sector Borrowing Requirement (PSBR). These long term omos absorbed liquidity from the financial system. Instead of selling more Treasury bills than were needed to meet the short term financial needs of the government, and thereby creating liquidity shortages, the Bank was selling more bonds than were needed, with a similar result. In order to ease the liquidity shortage the Bank became an active buyer of Treasury and, given the relative scarcity of the latter, commercial bills, at prices largely of its own choosing. Commercial bills were bought in such quantities that the prudence of the Bank sitting on a pile of company debt, for which the banking system was liable, especially at a time when business bankruptcies were at record levels, was questioned. It was also noted that 'overfunding' might affect the term structure of interest rates, by raising long term rates relative to short term rates in order to sell bonds in sufficient quantities. A significant feature of the 'overfunding' approach to monetary control was that the discount market had been largely redundant, except as a market maker for commercial bills, because the Bank has not been engineering liquidity shortages through short term omos. The 'overfunding' approach relied heavily on generating expectations that interest rates would fall so that capital gains could be made, the so-called Grand Old Duke of York strategy. It is clearly not always possible to generate such expectations, in which case more traditional methods of monetary control, involving perhaps short term omos, have to be relied upon. To the extent that 'overfunding' does raise long term interest rates, relative to their 'normal' levels, and to the extent that long term interest rates influence investment, the policy would, if pursued for a long period, have damaging effects on the economy.

The 'overfunding' method of monetary control was dropped following an announcement of the Chancellor in his 1985 Mansion House speech. He stated that issues of bonds would, in future, match funding needs. This announcement followed growing evidence that the Bank's willingness to buy commercial bills was distorting the financial system. The banks were only supposed to accept bills which were designed to fund commercial needs. There was accumulating evidence that many companies were issuing bills, and effectively raising funds from the

Bank, which were used for financial operations, often involving 'round tripping', rather than for commercial purposes. The Bank subsequently announced that it would attempt to reduce the 'bill mountain' over a period of time. Hopes that this would lead to reintermediation of business between banks and their customers may, however, be dashed by the introduction of the sterling commercial paper market in 1986 (15).

The 1970s were, therefore, a period in which changing methods of monetary control affected the development of the banking system. The ending of the interest rate cartel ushered in a period of increased competition between the major clearing banks. It followed a period in which there had been a fairly clear demarcation between the activities of the various types of bank (16) and other deposit taking institutions. Towards the end of the 1960s credit controls had been tight and the clearing banks and finance houses bore the brunt of the credit controls. Consequently normal banking business was diverted to the fringe banks (17), which often made loans and granted credit secured on second mortgages. CCC aimed to eliminate these distortions, by removing distortionary credit controls and by generating more competition in the banking sector. The new regime was expected to cause a contraction of the fringe banking sector, as normal clearing bank business was re-intermediated. In the event economic conditions (18) offset any success CCC may have had in this direction.

The booming property sector, which the clearing banks were discouraged from entering, provided ample opportunities for fringe, or secondary, banks to expand, despite some loss of traditional banking business to the clearers. The secondary banks drew increasingly on the rapidly growing wholesale money markets, in which commercial companies and major institutional investors were large depositors. The clearing banks, being excluded from the property market business and with industry undemanding, also lent funds through the interbank market. The major clearers did, however, deal in the property markets indirectly, through subsidiaries and the purchase of interest in fringe banks. The secondary banks were lending short term funds for long and medium terms. When economic conditions deteriorated in 1973 and sterling faced a crisis, interest rates were raised and the 'corset' was imposed. The Secondary Banking Crisis (19) resulted. The Bank launched the 'lifeboat', which effectively involved the sharing of lender of last resort responsibilities with the clearing banks. The effects of the crisis were still being felt at the end of the 1970s. The crisis ultimately induced an extension of the Bank's supervisory responsibilities, to cover licensed deposit takers (LDTs) as well as 'recognised banks', under the 1979 Banking Act (20).

The 1970s, therefore, marked the beginning of the breakdown of the traditional demarcations in the financial sector as the clearing banks, through subsidiaries and participation, diversified into new business. They developed major interests in finance houses, which were then primarily providers of consumer instalment credits, and related activities such as leasing and factoring. The spur to diversification was competition and the restrictions imposed by the 'corset' and qualitative credit controls. Traditional business developments were restricted by the 'corset' and the banks looked for new opportunities.

Not only did the clearing banks need to develop new products to attract and retain corporate business but they also faced growing competition for their retail business. Building society branch networks were growing apace and were attracting savings which might otherwise have been deposited in banks. The building societies paid interest net of a composite tax rate and the banks felt that this gave them a competitive edge. In addition, commercial banks outside the CLCB, such as the TSBs, the Yorkshire and Co-operative banks, the Scottish banks, and the National Girobank, also became significant competitors, especially in the retail banking market. Further, since 1973 especially, the internationalisation of the banking system had brought with it a growing presence of foreign banks in the City of London. These mainly competed for corporate and international business.

Clearly concerned by these developments, the CLCB began to demand the creation of a 'level playing field' (21). CCC had extended reserve requirements to other commercial banks and some other financial institutions. The 1981 "Provisions" had then extended cash deposit requirements to the wider banking sector. The CLCB, however, felt that further measures were required to achieve an environment free from government sanctioned competitive inequalities. The building societies had begun to develop their retail banking and money transmission services further in the early 1980s and continued to attract deposits at an alarming rate, from the CLCB's point of view. The government's 1984 (22) proposals for reforming the building societies by allowing them to offer, amongst other things, a wider array of traditional retail banking services, such as cheque guarantee cards and unsecured loans, also caused them concern. The CLCB campaigned for the abolition of the building societies' composite tax rate. In the event the 1984 Budget extended composite rate taxing to interest paid by the banks. The banks also responded to competition from building societies by launching an assault, in the early 1980s, on their traditional preserve, the home loans market. They had realised that by developing contacts with customers, through the provision of home loans, they could cross sell other financial services. The opportunities for cross selling, it soon became evident, would include not only traditional retail banking services but also other financial services, such as insurance. Lloyds Bank went even further and developed the Black Horse estate agency service. The building societies have long been associated with the estate agency and insurance business and the new legislation on building societies (23) permits them to extend their activities in these areas further.

On the commercial side the major clearing banks, having already developed merchant banking subsidiaries, decided to take further steps towards diversification, after 1983, in the lead up to the Big Bang (24). Most of them have supplemented their merchant banking interests with acquisitions of and participations in stock broking and jobbing firms and NatWest and Barclays have formally developed investment banking divisions. Thus the major clearers have developed, during the 1970s and 1980s, from fairly traditional commercial banks, concentrating on retail and corporate banking business, towards universal banks in the German mould. This development looks likely to progress even further as banks continue to move into business traditionally undertaken by non-bank financial institutions. Financial conglomerates are developing which aim to offer a whole array of financial services through financial supermarkets. Meanwhile, many of the merchant banks have been transforming themselves into investment banks to put them in a position to compete, after the Big Bang, with their American and Japanese cousins. Alongside the financial supermarkets and the investment banks there may still be room for some 'financial boutiques', through which smaller financial institutions can offer specialised services. Only time will tell whether the competition that will ensue after the Big Bang will further encourage these developments or whether it will, following a series of disappointments, lead to a retreat by some institutions into more traditional business.

The discount market meanwhile faces an uncertain future. Since the early 1970s the discount houses have widened the scope of their market making, and other more peripheral, services. They deal heavily in commercial bills, for example, in addition to their more traditional Treasury bill business and aim to increase their role in short term bond dealing after the Big Bang. They also hope to become major players in the nascent commercial paper market (25), should it take off. Their role as intermediaries between the Bank and the banks, in the former's pursuit of monetary policy, became less crucial during the early 1980s, especially during the period of 'overfunding'. The uncertainty was heightened in July 1986, when the Bank announced that it was going to remove the 'club money' requirement on the UK banks prior to the Big Bang. The banks will instead be required to adhere to new liquidity requirements (26). The end of 'club money' will deprive the discount houses of a plentiful supply of cheap funds from the banks and could reduce their profits. Their diversification has, however, made them less reliant upon it. Some commentators feel that the time is fast approaching when the Bank will interact more directly with the banks, through the medium of the interbank market.

The major clearing banks, meanwhile, are likely to face increasing competition not just from building societies and aggressive foreign banks such as Citibank, which is building up its UK and worldwide operations, but also for the TSB, which was finally (27) floated on the Stock Exchange in September 1986. The massive capital injection it has gained will widen its opportunities beyond its sound retail and nascent corporate business, significantly. A longer term matter for concern is the return of a Labour government whose current proposals for the financial system include (28): the creation of a National Investment Bank, to which the clearing banks may be expected to contribute funds; and the formation of a nationalised clearing bank, perhaps by merging the Post Office Saving Bank and the National Girobank, to compete with the major clearers. In the mid 1980s, however, banks were enjoying more freedom than at any time since the war, due to a series of 'deregulatory' measures and developments in the spheres of monetary control methods and monetary policy.

In 1969 the UK negotiated a conditional loan with the IMF, in order to help it through its balance of trade, and consequent exchange rate, difficulties. The 'letter of intent' (29) committed the UK to adopt, for a short period, targets for Domestic Credit Expansion (DCE) (30). Then in 1976, again as a result of negotiating a conditional loan with the IMF, Chancellor Dennis Healey announced target growth rates for sterling M3 and DCE. Since then, each year, successive Chancellors have announced target ranges for the rate of growth of the money supply. The record in hitting the targets has been rather poor (31) and various monetary aggregates have been targeted, ranging from the narrowest M0 to the widest PSL2. Often more than one monetary aggregate has been targeted. Experience has led to the growing suspicion that any monetary aggregate chosen for targeting will eventually become a 'wayward mistress' (32). The 1984 Financial Statement set target ranges for the growth of M0, a narrow money aggregate, and sterling M3, a broader money aggregate (33). Sterling M3 had been the only aggregate targeted consistently since 1976, but even its target was temporarily dropped following the Chancellor's October 1985 Mansion House speech. Sterling M3 was reinstated in the March 1986 Budget, with a higher and wider range. The targeting of M0 continued throughout 1985 and 1986.

The monetary policy of the Thatcher governments is embodied in the "Medium Term Financial Strategy", which was introduced in the 1980 Red Book (34). The aim of the MTFS is to reduce the rate of growth of the money supply progressively, year by year, with a view to reducing the inflation rate. Initially the goal seemed to be to reduce the inflation rate to the level experienced by the UK's major industrial competitor countries. Chancellor Lawson, in his first year of office (35), has, however, expressed a desire to see inflation reduced to zero. Broader aims of the strategy are to reduce the rate of interest and the tax rate, in order to stimulate growth. To achieve these objectives, the 1980 Financial Statement argued that the PSBR must be reduced (36). Finally, to achieve the reduction in the PSBR and to leave room for tax cuts, government expenditure, as a percentage of national expenditure, had to be reduced.

The PSBR includes: borrowing to service the National Debt; borrowing to meet the fiscal deficit between tax revenue and government expenditure; and borrowing to finance local authorities and nationalised industries. Concentrating initially on the fiscal deficit, this can be financed in a number of ways. Broadly speaking, the options are: to borrow short term on the UK money markets; to borrow long term in the bonds market; to formally borrow from abroad on either a short term or a long term basis, for example from commercial banks, the IMF, and the Eurobond market; and to try to attract capital inflows to the financial markets, as the US successfully did in the early 1980s. In the latter case foreign funds supplement domestic funds in financing the deficit through short and long term borrowing. These methods of financing the fiscal deficit are not mutually exclusive and in practice the deficit is financed through some mix of the sources outlined. A country attempting to control the money supply will try to avoid short term domestic borrowing, especially from banks, because it is tantamount to increasing the money supply. The Thatcher administration has also committed itself to reducing foreign indebtedness and so the option of borrowing directly from abroad has been ignored and contribution from this source, to the financing of the fiscal deficit, has been negative. Thus the only source of finance remaining was long term borrowing on the bond market. This has the drawback of pushing up long term interest rates, if the deficit is substantial and persistent, and this runs counter to the MTFS. Thus if interest rates are to be reduced, the fiscal deficit must be reduced, and, if taxes are to be reduced, government expenditure must be reduced. We have not got the space to enter into the debate concerning the economic logic of the MTFS; we shall instead only dwell briefly on its more obvious shortcomings.

The first shortcoming of the MTFS was that its targets for the reduction of the PSBR, and especially its fiscal deficit component, did not take account of the business cycle. The downswing of the business cycle would be expected to cause a reduction in tax revenue and an increase in government welfare expenditure, with the reverse effect occurring in the upswing. This was observed, at the time, by one of the instigators of the MTFS, Nigel Lawson, who was then serving as a junior minister in the Treasury. This shortcoming made it difficult to assess the government's success in pursuing the goals of the strategy, especially those of reducing the PSBR and government expenditure as a percentage of national income, in the ensuing recession of the early 1980s. A second criticism involves the rigidity of the strategy given the inherent uncertainty involved in the flow of North Sea oil revenue which was clearly expected to have a significant influence on the PSBR in the years following the inception of the MTFS.

In the event the PSBR overshot its targets, as did the government expenditure component, despite the government's expenditure 'cuts', which tended to hit capital programmes most heavily. Additionally, despite large increases in oil revenue, the tax burden was raised, rather than reduced, as a net result of the budgets through to 1985 - although some reduction was achieved in the 1985 budget and further tax cuts were promised for the 1987 budget. Each year most of the monetary aggregates overshot their target ranges as well. M0 has, however, proved to be an exception. In addition base drift (37) has been allowed, so that monetary growth overshooting has been treated as a bygone. Consequently, the MTFS targets for PSBR and government expenditure, and its components, and the monetary aggregates have had to be revised in each budget.

The overshooting of the PSBR targets has been attributed to the fact that the recession was much deeper, and unemployment growth more persistent, than anticipated. It has also been argued that this was partly the fault of the government, which pursued inappropriately tight monetary policy and forced up interest rates at a time when sterling was adopting the mantle of a petrocurrency, with the rise in North Sea oil production and the contribution that this was expected to make to the balance of trade. The net result was that sterling became overvalued and British industry suffered a severe loss of competitiveness. The overshooting of the monetary targets is partially explicable, via the government financing equation, by the overshooting in the PSBR. There was also the problem of reintermediation, following the removal of the 'corset'. In the post 1981 period there was a suggestion that the government had eased up on its monetary policy in order to bring down interest rates and improve the competitiveness of British industry by allowing a depreciation in sterling. The Chancellor, Nigel Lawson, also had to overcome the handicap of the pre-election spending spree, by government departments, in the run up to the 1983 election, in order to achieve a satisfactory outcome concerning the MTFS targets set in 1983.

In his 1983 Mansion House speech, Chancellor Lawson clarified the government's position on monetary policy. He stated that the monetary authorities were pursuing a policy of setting announced monetary growth targets whilst trying to keep both interest and exchange rates within unpublished bands. He also indicated that M0, which is close to widely accepted definitions of the monetary base, would be an important element of future monetary policy. This led to speculation that the Treasury at least (38) was considering a move to some variant of monetary base control. Although M0 has continued to be targeted in the budgets up to and including 1986, no moves toward base control have yet been made and the markets have proved sceptical about M0's usefulness as an indicator of monetary policy.

Subsequent monetary policy statements by the Chancellor, in Mansion House speeches and budget statements, have gradually increased the status of exchange rates, relative to monetary aggregates, as indicators of monetary policy. The 1985 Mansion House speech and 1986 Budget statements made it clear that sterling M3 in particular was no longer as reliable an indicator of monetary policy as it had been previously and the significance of its targeting should be downgraded. One reason given for this was that financial deregulation had made money aggregates which, like sterling M3, contain both interest and non-interest bearing components more difficult to interpret. Money used for transactions purposes, which had previously been held in non-interest bearing current accounts, was increasingly being held in interest bearing accounts and often not with banks but with other institutions, such as building societies. Further, falling inflation and the persistence of high nominal and, therefore, real interest rates was increasing the demand for liquidity. The rise in liquidity being indicated by the growth of the broader monetary aggregates need not, therefore, necessarily be interpreted as a rise in inflationary potential. The Bank, however, remained wary of the build up of liquidity, fearing that a change in economic conditions, such as the rise in inflation forecast for 1987 and a fall in nominal and real interest rates, might reverse the trend. A future fall in the demand for liquidity might consequently lead to a rapid build up in inflationary pressure. The high liquidity also increased the risks of a sterling crisis. A hint of trouble, perhaps in the run up to an election, might lead to a switch of funds abroad, by large companies for example. The company sector had also built up its liquidity in the mid 1980s.

Despite the promotion of the exchange rate as an indicator of monetary policy, no targets were announced. The Chancellor seemed to be adopting a favourable attitude towards joining the Exchange Rate Mechanism (ERM) (39) of the European Monetary System in 1986. This would effectively involve formal exchange rate targeting. Membership of the ERM was, however, opposed by the Prime Minister, who felt that the time for entry was not ripe. Following doubts about the government's commitment to its monetary policy, minor sterling crises occurred in January 1985 and January 1986. Each time the Bank had to raise interest rates to protect sterling. These episodes have left UK interest rates, in both real and nominal terms, high in relation to those prevailing in other major industrial countries and caused the pound to be overvalued, in the estimation of the Confederation of British Industry (CBI) and many other people. The emphasis of the anti-inflationary strategy, therefore, seemed to have shifted back to that prevailing in the early 1980s, which had proved to be successful in reducing inflation. With commodity prices falling and the pound appreciating relative to the dollar, in terms of which most internationally traded commodities are priced, import prices have been falling and imparting a beneficial effect to the inflation rate. The factor causing most concern, with regard to future inflation prospects, had become wage inflation because UK wage rates continued to increase faster than prices. The Chancellor seemed to hope that a high exchange rate would harden management resolve against granting inflationary wage increases, despite their high and rising profitability, by increasing competitive pressures in both the export markets and the domestic markets, from imported manufactured products. The exchange rate policy was, therefore, being used to condition wage settlements in place of an incomes policy.

It is not clear that this policy emphasis can be pursued in the long term. The CBI has repeatedly drawn attention to the damaging effects that high interest and exchange rates were having on its competitive position and its survey results, published in July 1986, showed a fall in orders in general and export orders in particular. Further, the rapid fall in oil prices since the beginning of 1986 had led to a significant reduction in the visible trade balance and it became clear that, even if the invisible trade surplus achieved the levels forecast, somewhat optimistically many commentators felt, by the Treasury, the balance of payments might well move into a deficit in 1986. At any rate, the surplus would be significantly less than forecast. The fall in oil prices and declining balance of payments prospects were, therefore, likely to cause sterling to depreciate to more competitive levels. Unless the Chancellor wished to raise interest rates further, relative to the other industrial countries, the policy seemed to have a limited life. The significant tax cuts promised for the 1987 Budget were also brought into doubt by the government's reduced oil revenues, the continued rise in unemployment, and political pressure to improve the health and education services. The option of ERM membership remained and so did that of monetary base control, although, as long as M0 continued to grow within its target band, this was effectively in operation as a medium term policy anyway. The Conservative government was unlikely to countenance an incomes policy but had adopted a longer term policy of encouraging profit related pay and wider share ownership. It was hoped that, amongst other things, this would increase workers' appreciation of 'reasonable' wage demands.

There has been some criticism that the MTFS targets would have been more seriously breached, since 1982, had the government not pursued a revenue generating privatisation programme (40). Expected revenue from sales of shares in nationalised industries have not been adequately spelt out in statements concerning MTFS targets and, perhaps, should have been. The privatisation programme and the price rises imposed, on gas and electricity for example, in the public sector can be seen in the broader context of attempts to reduce the subsidisation, of nationalised industry, component of the PSBR.

The government also proved innovative in seeking out alternative sources of borrowing, especially from small savers. Index linked National Savings Certificates and bonds were introduced, for example, and the National Savings Bank has generally become a more aggressive competitor, for small savings, with banks and building societies. The 1984 Budget, which imposed composite tax deduction on banks to bring them in line with building societies, should also help the National Savings Bank attract small savers since it does not have to deduct the composite tax rate from its interest payments.

Thus, the emphasis on exchange rates, rather than monetary aggregates, complemented the methods of monetary control in leaving the banks virtually free from government interference in the mid 1980s.

There were of course the necessary prudential requirements, imposed by the Bank on capital and liquidity, but these were generally accepted as fair and necessary. The banks were being permitted to explore new business opportunities, especially those opened up by the removal of exchange controls (41) and the Big Bang (42) and the government was actively promoting London as a financial centre and attempting to create a 'level playing field' for financial institutions. Despite increased competition, from foreign banks, building societies and the smaller clearing banks, the major clearing banks were achieving record profit levels. They were even winning back some of the lost ground in retail banking, from the building societies in particular. The commercial paper market, introduced in 1986, raised the possibility that some of their corporate business would be lost but opened up opportunities for fee earning business. Their only remaining concern seemed to be the perennial threat that the next budget would include a special tax on their profits. The previous Chancellor, Geoffrey Howe, had hit them with a windfall profits tax and Chancellor Lawson was likely to be short of sufficient revenue, due to the oil price collapse in 1986, to permit the tax cuts promised for the 1987 Budget. He had already damaged banks' profits following the 1984 Budget, when he had reduced tax allowances relating to their leasing business and called for payment of tax on previous revenues, and was known to have considered introducing a special financial services tax whilst formulating his 1986 Budget.

A change in the emphasis of monetary policy, however, seemed imminent and further consideration might have to be given to effective monetary control methods following the Big Bang and the ending of 'overfunding'. Membership of the ERM would, for example, mean that the UK monetary policy would have to be as tight as that pursued by the Bundesbank and monetary control methods might have to be revised to facilitate this. Additionally, the Chancellor may not yet have given up the idea of introducing more formal monetary base control. In the near future, at least until a Labour government is returned, the banks are, however, likely to continue to enjoy their relative freedom from government credit controls and directives. In the light of this emerging freedom and the government's commitment to promoting competition and creating a 'level playing field' in the financial sector, the dominance of the UK clearing system by the major clearing banks seemed incongruous. Reform of the clearing system is discussed in the next section.

2.2 **Reforming the Clearing System**

The members of the Bankers Clearing House (43) (BCH) published proposals for extending the membership of various parts of the clearing system in December 1984. The proposals are included in a review of the organisation, membership and control of payment clearing systems by a working party which commenced work in March 1984, following applications by Citibank and Standard Chartered Bank to become members of the BCH. Citibank and Standard Chartered agreed to defer their applications until after the report (44) and potential applicants were asked to do the same. The review aimed to take into account a number of reports which had commented on the clearing system, and recent developments in banking technology.

(i) **The Price Commission (PC) Report (1978)** (45). The PC's review of Money Transmission Services (MTS) deals mainly with the charging system for current account related services and for currency distribution. Apart from noting its observations: that provision of MTS is an integral part of clearing bank business, enabling them to raise funds largely in the form of current accounts; that competition in the provision of MTS had increased since the 1967 report of the National Board of Prices and Incomes (46) but was still imperfect; and that in most respects the MTS offered by UK banks compared favourably with their counterparts in other countries; we shall concentrate on its comments on the BCH.

The PC noted that the members of the Committee of London Clearing Bankers (47) (CLCB) had effective control of the clearing system and that no comparable cheque clearing system existed or was likely to exist, given the efficiency of the system and the expense of establishing an alternative. This was tantamount to claiming that cheque clearing was a natural monopoly since it implied that the CLCB was providing clearing services efficiently on a downward sloping average cost curve, so that there were barriers to entry through economies of scale. The implication was that the London Clearing Banks had formed a sort of cartel in order to produce an efficient clearing system of sufficient scale to meet demand. It was not that they had exploited their position to make maximum profits. It was further observed that the BCH had proved willing to accept new members (48) and had even offered membership to other banks (49); that the terms for membership did not appear unreasonable; and that it was a non-profit making organisation, sharing costs between members in proportion to usage, with non-members having access by using members as agents. It was, however, felt that more could be done to overcome the impression that the BCH was being used to restrict competition from newcomers to retail banking.

The PC argued that the BCH was a national resource, despite being owned by the CLCB. The implication here is that there is something infrastructural about the clearing system, making it essential to the workings of a modern society, like telephone and electricity networks for example. Not surprisingly, therefore, it proposed that regulation of admission to the BCH should lie in the hands of the authorities, who should also arbitrate in disputes concerning allocation of costs, should they arise. It was felt that the Bank of England would be the appropriate authority, given the power with which it was endowed through the 1946 Act (50). It proposed that banks admitted to the BCH should be given seats on the Board of the BCH. Finally, the PC acknowledged that the CLCB had in general taken a responsible line in representing the retail banking industry, but noted that any tendency in the direction of a cartel would be moderated if full membership of the CLCB were open to all substantial retail banking institutions.

(ii) **The Wilson Report (WR) (1980)** (51). The WR noted that: the provision of MTS was one of the three main functions of clearing banks (52) and that they depend on it to generate their deposit base; it was a market which they dominated (53) and that since 1971 (54) there had been an increase in competition in the provision of MTS.

It was observed that the provision of MTS is an area in which a significant degree of co-operation is needed, because operating efficiency and the containment of costs require a high degree of standardisation of procedures; that "the central clearing infrastructure has something of the characteristics of a natural monopoly"; that in many other countries it was publicly owned, with payments services being provided by private banks; and that central banks in other countries are often more involved in clearing non-cash payments, than in the UK.

It was noted that the clearing banks claimed to have fully recognised the need for co-operation, to avoid socially wasteful competition and to exploit the technical opportunities increasingly available (55). No evidence was found to suggest that banks had used ownership of the clearing system to impose unreasonable conditions on their competitors and so restrict competition from newcomers to retail banking. It was noted that non-members had access through agency arrangements with members.

It was, however, stated that "had we been starting anew, there might have been some attraction in a publicly owned central clearing system", but that prevailing arrangements appeared to be working satisfactorily and there was little reason to expect that public ownership would increase efficiency. This indicates that it was believed that the 'natural monopoly' was operating near to the average cost pricing condition that might be imposed, under regulation, to prevent excess profits. Given that regulation can sometimes inhibit technical change and reduce the incentive for cost reduction (56), then regulation in this case appeared unnecessary.

Finally, because of the strength of public interest in the clearing system and to avoid suspicion of clearing banks abusing their position, it was recommended that the Bank of England should become more closely involved in regulating admission to the BCH. It does, however, draw attention to the possible conflict of interest arising out of the Bank's membership of the BCH by virtue of its role as government's banker. It suggests that the conflict of interest could best be adjudicated upon by an outside body.

(iii) **The National Consumer Council (NCC) Report (1983)** (57). In 1982 the Office of Fair Trading (OFT) canvassed more than 30 non-clearing banks and found no complaints about agency arrangements and no advocates of direct access to clearing. It then obtained a direction from the Secretary of State for Trade and Industry discharging the Director General of the OFT from his statutory obligation to refer registered restrictive practice agreements, in this case the clearing arrangements, to the Restrictive Practices Court for investigation. In contrast, the NCC found a couple of banks and a major building society who were unhappy about agency arrangements, two of them complaining vigorously.

The NCC argued that cheque clearing was a natural monopoly, like the clearing system for electronic payments which grew out of it, in the sense that, like the telephone system, everyone who subscribes to the system has an interest in seeing that everyone is connected to the same system. This is not necessarily directly related to the economic definition of natural monopoly referred to earlier, but catches the flavour of a commonsense or literal understanding of the term. It implies that the clearing system is infrastructural and should be viewed as a public utility, in which case it is not desirable to have parallel networks. The 'naturalness' of the monopoly thus arises out of social considerations concerning the efficiency derived from having a unified clearing system, rather than from economies of scale per se. The NCC observes that, in principle, there are powerful arguments against such a system being jointly owned by a small group who provide the service and that joint ownership enables the CLCB member banks to dictate terms of entry to organisations wishing to join, by determining criteria for acceptability.

It is noted in particular that non-members of Bankers' Automated Clearing Services (BACS) (58) suffer a disadvantage when competing for accounts of the hitherto unbanked employees (59) and that this may well have a detrimental effect on the growth of building society account holding.

The NCC considered two alternative forms of organisation: requiring the clearing banks to sell ownership of the BCH and BACS to a group of financial institutions not directly interested in providing MTS themselves - clearing would then be operated as a commercial service and would be institutionally distinct from ownership and control of the system; and the extension of ownership along the lines of the Canadian Payments Association, through which ownership and control has been removed from the clearing banks exclusively and transferred to a new 'umbrella' body. In the former case, it was felt that the Bank of England might need to have an interest: to ensure that the terms of entry were appropriate; and to monitor the credentials of entrants carefully, in accordance with its supervisory responsiblities.

The NCC Report concluded that the accumulated evidence of previous reports and the NCC findings did not justify a recommendation that, at the time, the clearing system should be removed from clearing bank ownership. It observed, however, that there were revolutionary changes occurring in the market for personal banking, including: the move by building societies into the business of providing MTS (60); pressures to encourage cashless pay; and the introduction of the new Electronic Funds Transfer (EFT) technology. The latter, it argued, should not be the exclusive preserve of existing clearing banks and should not be made available to other financial institutions on terms convenient to the clearing banks. In such an environment, it proposed that the attitude of the clearing banks to new competition should be monitored by the government. With this in mind, the NCC recommended that the government should announce its intention to review the development of MTS provision within two or three years following the Report. If any evidence of exclusion of competition were then found, it should consider whether joint ownership of the clearing systems by the members of the CLCB was appropriate. The government made no such announcement but the BCH review was announced within a year of the NCC Report and probably pre-empted it.

In the NCC Report (61), it was observed that functional membership of the BCH was open to any cheque issuing bank which, among other things, issues 1% of the total number of cheques processed by the BCH. It was argued that this was a higher hurdle than it appeared. The Co-operative Bank only just met this requirement and the National Girobank did not qualify on this score, but was nevertheless admitted. Other requirements for membership (62) were: an existing branch network; acceptance of the cost of participation; and ability to conform to the functional requirements and timetable of the clearing system. The Co-operative Bank, the Central Trustee Savings Bank (CTSB) and the National Girobank all became functional members of the BCH and sponsoring or second line members of BACS.

Finally, it was noted that the numbers of consumers able to use Electronic Funds Transfer at Point of Sale (EFTPOS) would be greatly increased if the accounts of non-bank financial intermediaries, such as building societies, could also be debited through the system.

(iv) **<u>The Child Report and Proposals (1984)</u>** (63). The Child Report introduced the main principles of a new organisational structure, pointing out that detailed work would be required to translate the principles into rules and regulations for the various components of the new structure. The working party aimed to develop a structure to: maintain the integrity and effectiveness of clearing; accommodate criticisms of current arrangements; and create a robust flexible structure able to maintain efficiency in the face of extended ownership and changing technology.

It recommended that the new structure should consist of: an umbrella organisation, set up as an unincorporated business, to oversee the development of the clearing and payments industry; and three limited companies. The latter would cover: general clearing and credit clearing (paper bulk clearing); high value clearing (CHAPS (64) and town clearing); and electronic bulk clearing (BACS Ltd).

The umbrella organisation would be effectively a trade association, representing and overseeing the payments industry. Membership should consist of settlement members of the individual clearing companies and associate members, who would use the facilities on an agency basis, providing that they are appropriately regulated.

Membership of the separate companies would be open to all appropriately registered institutions which meet explicit objective criteria, including: compliance with technical and operational requirements; maintenance of settlement facilities with the Bank of England; payment of a fair share of running costs and a fair entry price; and the meeting of the minimum value requirement discussed below.

It was believed that the proposed broad membership of the umbrella organisation would satisfy past criticisms regarding alleged secrecy and lack of consultation, the distinction between shareholding and non-shareholding members having been removed (65). Further, ownership and control of the individual companies was to be placed in the hands of all members, replacing the previous two tier system of membership (66).

The admissions criteria were ostensibly designed to allow expansion of membership without undermining the integrity and efficiency of clearings. It was hoped that group settlement membership and consideration of potential, rather than actual, clearing volumes would go a long way towards satisfying criticisms of the exclusivity of the prevailing arrangements.

It was noted that the impact on membership would vary between clearings. In paper bulk clearings, only the Yorkshire Bank could meet the new actual volume criteria, which was to be ½% of the combined clearing volume, although one or two financial institutions might be able to do so on a potential volume or group settlement basis. It is worth noting, however, that provision was made for the possibility that membership could be reviewed, in the light of actual clearing volume. The main implication for BACS will be the extension of share ownership amongst the existing members. In CHAPS, twenty five additional, to the ten member, banks might be able to meet the volume criteria (67), including Citibank and Standard Chartered. As regards associate membership, there are approximately 200 banks with agency facilities in paper clearing and 200 building societies are sponsored users of BACS, making a total of approximately 400 eligible associate members.

Citibank and Standard Chartered could, therefore, join CHAPS and the umbrella organisation, provided they established settlement facilities with the Bank of England and were willing to abide by the other entry requirements including payment of their share of operating costs and payment of the admission charge, i.e. the price of buying shares in capital commensurate with clearing volume. This they in fact did in 1985. Applications are also invited from other prospective settlement members and associate members. Criteria for entry for the latter include: prudential supervision by an appropriate body; an agency or similar arrangement with a settlement member of at least one clearing; and willingness to pay an annual fee to cover administration costs.

It was hoped that the umbrella organisation would oversee the planning of the new MTS, especially those which might involve a large number of financial institutions, such as EFTPOS, but it was acknowledged that it would not have a monopoly of planning and development rights in this area and that initiatives might be taken by outside groups of financial institutions.

(v) **Answering the Critics**. Appendix 1 of the Child Report attempts to answer the various criticisms of the clearing system contained in the reports reviewed above. It acknowledges the high efficiency of the clearing system, taking it as read. Little evidence concerning criteria for judging its efficiency is presented. It notes that the reports reviewed above suggest that continued domination of the clearing system by the large clearing banks might be detrimental but draws attention to the fact that new entrants, namely the CTSB, the Co-operative Bank and the National Girobank, have become members of the clearing system since 1970.

It is argued that the notion that the clearing system is a natural monopoly is spurious. In support of this proposition it cites the existence of two or more rival clearing systems in a number of countries which do not suffer major duplication of infrastucture or operating inefficiency. It is argued that the British system can be considered to be a national resource only in the sense that it is available for use on a nationwide basis and that, because the clearing system has been developed with private risk capital, it is inappropriate to regard it as some kind of public utility. It is, however, noted that, although scope for competition within the existing system is limited, it should not be inferred that clearing is a natural monopoly or national resource. Instead, it implies that the system has operated efficiently and equitably. This is evidenced by offers of membership to suitable banks in the past, some of which had been declined (68). It is pointed out that agency services are provided, by settlement members, and charged for, on a competitive basis.

(vi) **Payments Systems Abroad** (69). The international survey of clearing systems, in Appendix 2 of the Child Report, finds considerable variation in payments clearing systems and in the role of the central banks in those systems, reflecting mainly historical factors relating to the evolution of each country's banking and financial system. It is noted that differences in financial structure have become less pronounced in recent years and that there is evidence of convergence in the structure of national payments systems, with the advent of electronic technology reinforcing this trend. Payments systems, it is observed, have evolved in various countries in response to market requirements and technological developments, largely in an ad hoc manner and with limited planning and involvement by public authorities. Increasingly, however, the complexity of the alternative delivery systems has forced the main participants in the national payments system to pay greater attention to the need for closer co-ordination of the operations of existing clearing systems and future developments. Implicit in its comments on the various countries' systems is the view that inefficiency results from duplication and lack of co-ordination.

In countries with several co-existing payments

circuits, the circuits usually interface through bilateral arrangements or through central bank facilities. In such cases national central banks play an active part in bringing the various payments circuits together and supporting the creation of an integral payments system.

The review of the clearing systems in various other countries draws a number of conclusions, including: the advantages of integrated national systems are greater for electronic payments than for paper based payments systems; co-operation between rival systems appears to be essential but interface links can be provided either bilaterally or through central banks; electronic systems tend to have broader membership than paper based systems; the central bank or Ministry of Finance (70) plays a key co-ordinating role concerning the development of payments in many countries; only Canada has a formally established umbrella organisation; and the concept of separate clearings within an umbrella organisation, though present in a rudimental form in some countries, is not properly developed in any of the countries surveyed. The survey's findings seem to undermine the proposition that the payments system is not a natural monopoly, see Section (viii) below.

(vii) **The Payments System of the Future**. Finally, Appendix 3 of the Report contains a discussion of Electronic Funds Transfer at Point of Sale (EFTPOS), which is discussed more fully in the next chapter. It is noted: that the clearing banks have incurred costs and provided the impetus for its development over the last ten years and that they 'own' the work done so far on the development of the system; that the form of central organisation, which seems essential to administer the network, requires further considera-tion; and that questions of ownership of terminals and other equipment are still to be resolved and some matters remain an issue for resolution between consumers (cardholders) and retailers. It is pointed out that if ownership of the system were to be confined to the 'founding' banks, participation in the system would be likely to be wider. Non-clearing banks, non-bank financial intermediaries and retailers might also issue cards. Such participation would be a matter for negotiation between founding members and the issuing bodies or parties. Finally, it is observed that the rules governing membership and participation would depend, in part, on ownership but systems of membership could be envisaged along the lines of agency or sponsorship arrangements. These were to remain questions for discussion.

The Child Report makes provision for the establishment of a fourth clearing company, to deal with EFTPOS and related developments arising out of innovations in banking technology. This company would also be overseen by the umbrella organisation. If ownership of the company was initially confined to the 'founding banks', they would be able to recover some of the costs already incurred, in preparing the groundwork for a nationwide EFTPOS system, from the financial institutions joining the company at a later date.

(viii) **Assessment**. The proposals contained in the Child Report seem to be near to the minimum necessary to satisfy criticisms and comments, contained in the various reports reviewed above, concerning restriction on membership. The concept of separate clearings allows entry to the clearing system to be restricted to membership of only one of the companies in most cases. Entry requirements for the paper bulk clearing system are not markedly eased. The main effects are likely to be those of extending the membership of BACS and of the umbrella body. It may well be that true power will continue to reside with the big clearers through their dominance, by virtue of being the largest shareholders, of the operating companies.

It is to be noted that the requirement that members must have settlement accounts with the Bank of England introduces an additional hurdle and gives the Bank more effective supervisory powers over the clearing system. Additionally it is also to be a member of the umbrella organisation and the various companies, as of right. This seems to be in accordance with the various reports reviewing the clearing system.

The claim that the clearing system is not a natural monopoly does not seem to square with the view that the efficiency of the system rests, in part, on its nationwide coverage and that systems in other countries have increased efficiency by interfacing their various clearing systems, eliminating duplication, and co-ordinating future developments. There is perhaps some misunderstanding of the meaning of the term natural monopoly, as seemed to be the case in the NCC report. The commonsense meaning, based on the view that the clearing system is infrastructural or a national resource and should be regarded as a public utility, seems to have been adopted. Since public utilities are usually heavily regulated, if they remain in the private sector, or more commonly are part of the public sector, one can understand the clearing banks' concern over allegations that the clearing system is a natural monopoly. In economics, a natural monopoly is a monopoly that arises when there is only room in the market for one efficient firm to provide the required volume of services, or goods, given current market demand. Other firms entering on a lower scale would be operating at a significant cost disadvantage and would be unable to compete. There is thus a natural barrier to entry due to economies of scale. The discussion and observations in Appendices 1 and 2 of the Child Report seem to accord with the view that the clearing system is a natural monopoly in the economic sense, particularly in the case of electronic clearing. In cases of natural monopoly the market fails to regulate efficiently and the economic policy prescription is for the state either to regulate the prices of natural monopolies or to impose a credible threat of regulation, through anti-trust legislation. Such measures aim to prevent the natural monopolists from exploiting their monopoly positions and to ensure that they adopt average, or perhaps marginal, cost pricing. It is clear that such regulation need not entail public ownership, which the clearing banks clearly oppose.

As the Wilson Report implicitly observed, the clearing banks did not appear to be abusing their monopoly position, organised through an arrangement which is effectively a cartel in the supply of clearing services and which they felt obliged to register with the OFT as a restrictive practice, and did appear to be providing the service efficiently. Consequently, there appeared to be no need to regulate the monopoly. This is true because the threat of regulation, implicit in UK monopoly and restrictive practice legislation, is sufficient. But the risk of abuse remains, hence the suggestions by the NCC: that there should be increased involvement of the Bank, in a monitoring role; and that the threat of future investigation should be instigated. The most telling remark in the Wilson Report is the one that "if we had been starting anew there might be some attraction in a publicly owned clearing system". This seems to acknowledge that because the clearing banks have invested their own risk capital in establishing an efficient system to provide services which are essential for the pursuit of their legitimate business of attracting deposits, no change is needed and any change of ownership would perhaps be unfair. It is a bit worrying, however, that none of the reports present detailed empirical evidence concerning the generally accepted efficiency of the UK clearing system or of the comparative (in-)efficiency of those in other countries. The survey presented in Appendix 2 of the Child Report merely describes the structures of the systems in various countries. Little attempt is even made to evaluate whether geographic or demographic factors might influence the issue of whether one or more payment clearing systems might be required for efficiency.

(ix) **Conclusions**. In 1971, new monetary control arrangements, entitled "Competition and Credit Control" (71) (CCC), were introduced requiring the abolition of the interest rate cartel that had been operated by the London Clearing Banks. Also in the 1970s, other financial institutions, such as building societies, began to compete more actively in the retail banking market and there has been an internationalisation of banking which has significantly increased the scope of competition. Amidst all this change, the cartel-like arrangement of the clearing system remained. In the Child Report the banks responded finally to the various criticisms of this arrangement and introduced proposals for extending the membership of the clearing system. These proposals appear to be near to the minimum necessary to meet the criticisms and comments, concerning restriction of membership, contained in the reports reviewed in this chapter. They will, however, lead to a significantly wider membership of CHAPS and have resulted in the first foreign bank, namely Citibank, becoming a member of the clearing system (72). The proposals for the future development of the electronic payments system give some cause for concern, however, and we shall discuss this issue further in the next chapter.

Notes

1. Bank of England (1971).
2. Bank of England (1981b).
3. Bank Rate was the minimum rate of interest at which the Bank of England would normally lend to the discount houses. It was replaced by the Minimum Lending Rate in October 1982.
4. Balances placed with the Bank of England equal to a specified percentage of their eligible liabilities.
5. Eligible liabilities are, broadly speaking, a bank's sterling deposit liabilities, excluding deposits having an original maturity of over two years, and any sterling resources obtained by switching foreign currencies into sterling. Reserve assets comprise: balances with the Bank of England (excluding special deposits); money at call with the discount market and listed brokers, Treasury and eligible local authority and commercial bills; and short term government and nationalised industry stocks. See Bank of England (1971, 1981b) for details or Brown (1982, Appendicies II and III).
6. Committee of London Clearing Bankers (1978).
7. Command Paper 7858 (1980).
8. Monopolies Commission (1968).
9. They were the supervisory responsibility of the Department of Trade and Industry, see Chapter 5.
10. See Brown (1982) for a history of periods in which the 'corset' was in operation.
11. Command Paper 7858 (1980).
12. Bank of England (1981b).
13. See Chapter 5.
14. 'Round tripping' occurs when borrowers take advantage of an opportunity to utilise previously undrawn overdraft and credit facilities to relend at a profit, on the interbank and Eurocurrency markets for example.
15. See Chapter 1.
16. E.g. commercial and merchant.
17. Supervised by the Department of Trade and Industry rather than the Bank of England, see Chapter 5.
18. See Bank of England (1978).
19. See Reid (1982), Channon (1977) and Bank of England (1978).
20. See Chapter 5.
21. I.e. competition environment without government endowed tax and other privileges for certain groups of institutions.
22. Command Paper 9316 (1984).
23. Building Society Act (1986).
24. The reform of the Stock Exchange which came into effect in October 1986, see Chapter 4.
25. See Chapter 1.
26. See Chapter 5.
27. Following a series of challenges to the legality of the proposed flotation by depositor groups who believed that

the TSB was in fact owned by its depositors. The House of Lords eventually ruled in favour of the TSB in July 1986. The TSB was formally transferred to the private sector later in July as part of the procedure laid down under the 1985 Trustee Savings Bank Act to enable flotation.

28. See Chapter 6 for further discussion.

29. Which outlines the government's commitment to policy targets agreed with the IMF following negotiations.

30. The IMF's favoured measure of monetary growth, see Brown (1982) for a definition.

31. See Midland Bank Review (Autumn 1984) for a review of targets and outcomes up to 1984 and Economic Trends (CSO) for the most recent figures.

32. This has become known as Goodhart's Law.

33. M1 and PSL2, see Financial Statistics Explanatory Handbook (CSO) for definitions, have also been targeted under the MTFS, for a period, since 1979.

34. House of Commons (1980).

35. Nigel Lawson took over as Chancellor from Geoffrey Howe, following the 1983 post-election Cabinet reshuffle.

36. This argument was based on the view that the government faced a budget constraint which could be usefully formulated in terms of counterparts of sterling M3 growth, see Brown (1982, Appendix 1).

37. The practice of resetting targets for monetary aggregates, based on actual monetary outcomes, rather than previous target levels.

38. The Bank had made its opposition to the adoption of base control in the UK clear, see Bank of England (1979).

39. The ERM sets fixed bands within which participating countries' currencies can fluctuate against each other. Realignments are required when currencies can no longer be contained within the bands. The Treasury had opposed UK membership on a number of grounds, see Dennis and Nellis (1984). Their position seemed to have changed in 1986, although the Chancellor added the proviso that he only favoured entry when the time was ripe.

40. The proceeds from the privatisations were in fact counted effectively as negative expenditures. They consequently reduced the PSBR and were not counted as revenues for funding it.

41. In October 1979.

42. See Chapter 4.

43. The ten members of the BCH are: the Bank of England, the Barclays, Lloyds, Midlands, William and Glyn's, Co-operative, National Westminster and Central Trustee Savings banks; Coutts & Co., and the National Girobank. BCH Ltd is a service company that employs staff and owns premises for various purposes, including clearing operations to a small extent. It employs the Chief Inspector and staff to provide the limited central services required in paper clearings. It is

owned by the six banks whose Chairmen are members of the CLCB. The Board of BCH Ltd consists of the Chairmen of the owner banks.

44. Which has become known as the Child Report because the Chairman of the Working Party was Mr D.M. Child, Deputy Group Chief Executive, National Westminster Bank.

45. Banks: Charges for Monetary Transmission Services, Price Commission, HMSO, 17 April 1978.

46. Command Paper 3292, HMSO.

47. The members of the CLCB were the Chairmen of six banks; the Barclays, Lloyds, Midland, National Westminster and William and Glyn's banks and Coutts & Co. The CLCB was replaced by the CLSB (the Committee of London and Scottish Bankers) in 1985, after having been in existence for 160 years. The CLSB consists of the members of the CLCB plus the Chairmen of the two major Scottish clearing banks (the Bank of Scotland and the Royal Bank of Scotland, which merged with William and Glyn's in 1985, so that the latter is not separately represented) and Standard Chartered, which became a clearing bank following the Child Report.

48. In February 1974 the members of the CLCB agreed that the Co-operative Bank should have direct access to the clearing facilities and offered clearing agency facilities to other non-clearing institutions. As a result the Central Trustee Savings Bank also joined the BCH as a functional member in November 1975, and the National Girobank in March 1981.

49. The Yorkshire and the Scottish clearing banks decided not to join, as did the National Girobank initially.

50. Under Section 4 of the Bank of England Act 1946: "The Treasury may from time to time give such directions to the Bank as, after consultation with the Governor of the Bank, they think necessary in the public interest"; "The Bank, if they think it necessary in the public interest, may request information from and make recommendations to bankers, and may, if so authorised by the Treasury, issue directions to any banker for the purpose of securing that effect is given to any such request or recommendation."

51. Committee to Review the Functioning of Financial Institutions: Report, June 1980, Cmnd 7937, HMSO.

52. The other two being their deposit taking and lending functions.

53. In 1979, the London Clearing Banks accounted for 90% of non-cash payments. The London Clearing Banks were the six banks whose Chairmen form the CLCB; see note 46.

54. When "Competition and Credit Control" (CCC) was introduced, see Section 2.1.

55. See Committee of London Clearing Bankers (1978).

56. It is sometimes argued that regulated firms may be less interested in making technological innovations and in heading off cost increases than unregulated firms. This is because, with imposed average cost pricing, cost increases can

be passed on in higher prices, maintaining normal profit, and there is little incentive in reducing costs, since this will not lead to a rise in profits. Prices will merely fall in line with average costs, thus maintaining normal profits. Given the usual time lag in adjusting regulated prices, however, there may be an incentive to reduce costs, to make supra-normal profits in the short run, and to prevent cost increases, which would lead profits to fall below normal in the short run.

57. National Consumer Council (1983).

58. BACS was registered as a private limited liability company in September 1971. Its shareholders were: the Barclays, Lloyds, Midland, National Westminster and William & Glyn's banks. Loan capital was subscribed by the shareholding banks, the Bank of England, and the three Scottish clearing banks. Other banks participating in the system were: the Central Trustee Savings, the Co-operative, the Clydesdale and the Northern banks; the Bank of England; Coutts & Co.; the National Girobank; the Bank of Scotland and the Royal Bank of Scotland. These nine member banks, along with the five shareholding banks, would sponsor customers for direct input to BACS, and were called the sponsoring banks. The policy relating to the operations and development of BACS lay with its Board of Directors, which included representatives from each of the shareholding banks and the CLCB. There was also a consultative committee, which consisted of the representatives of the shareholding banks and of: the Bank of England, the Central Trustee Savings Bank, the Co-operative Bank, the National Girobank, and the Scottish clearing banks (1 representative).

59. Inter-Bank Research Organisation (1982) notes that the proportion of people paid weekly in cash had risen from 42%, in 1976, to 58%, in 1981, and that direct payment by Bank Giro Credit had risen from 26% to 38%. Clearly, financial intermediaries wish to encourage this trend since it is a major source of new accounts. It can, however, take at least a day longer for an employee's pay to reach his or her account in a building society, for example, via a BACS intermediary, than it will if the account is held with one of the BACS sponsoring members. This is disadvantageous because people naturally want access to their pay as soon as possible. See National Consumer Council (1983).

60. Many building societies were already offering cheque book accounts and providing MTS through Automated Teller Machines and a further extension of their MTS and other retail banking services has been permitted, by subsequent legislation, see Section 2.1 and Chapter 4.

61. See National Consumer Council (1983, Section 9, p. 136).

62. Identified by the Committee of London Clearing Bankers (1978).

63. Members of the Bankers Clearing House (1984).

64. CHAPS is the Clearing House Automated Payments

System. It is an electronic sterling transfer service which came into operation on 9 February 1984. It provides a nationwide alternative to the paper based town clearing system for transactions of £10,000 or over. It was developed by the 12 settlement banks: the Barclays, Lloyds, National Westminster, Midland, Co-operative, Clydesdale and Central Trustee Savings banks; the Banks of England and Scotland; the Royal Bank of Scotland group; the National Girobank; and Coutts & Co.; each of which holds accounts with the Bank of England for purposes of settling indebtedness. Over 50 non-settlement banks have arranged to send and/or receive payments through CHAPS. There was no central organisation to operate the system, instead a set of agreed rules were lodged with the Office of Fair Trading. There was, however, a policy committee comprising representatives from all the settlement banks, except the Clydesdale Bank and Coutts & Co.

65. The members of the CLCB (see note 47) were previously the main policy making group and the banks they represented owned BCH Ltd (see note 43). The proposed umbrella organisation will take over the CLCB's role of overseeing and representing the clearing system.

66. The previous two tier membership of BACS (described in note 58) and the BCH (described in Note 43), by virtue of the distinction between the BCH and BCH Ltd, was to be replaced by settlement membership for banks wishing to join and willing and able to meet the various entry requirements.

67. Namely that the bank should have a potential for at least ½% of the combined clearing volume covered by CHAPS Ltd.

68. See note 49.

69. See Bank for International Settlements (1985) for an alternative and more detailed survey.

70. Particularly in Japan.

71. See Bank of England (1971) and Section 2.1.

72. Although it is not to be a member of the CLSB, see note 47.

Chapter Three

THE DEVELOPMENT OF AN ELECTRONIC PAYMENTS SYSTEM IN THE UK

3.1 Introduction

At the outset it is worth noting that, despite the rapid growth in the use of cheques and plastic credit and debit cards, cash remains the dominant means of payment in the UK. The 'cashless society' is thus still a remote prospect. In 1981, nearly 90% of all payments of one pound or more and 86% of all payments of three pounds or more were made in cash (1).

The non-cash transactions system is largely based on Paper Funds Transfer (PFT). This operates primarily through the cheque clearing system rather than the Post Office Giro system, which was introduced in 1968 to provide a rapid, cheap and convenient alternative money transmission service. Perhaps due to its relatively late introduction, it has never reached the level of use typical in many continental European countries. The clearing banks had set up their own system, called Bank Giro Credits, nine years earlier. The banks' system is used largely by current account holders, to pay bills by attaching cheques. The growing costs involved in processing the massive amount of paper generated by the PFT system have forced banks to explore methods of cost reduction. These must involve a reduction in the amount of paper to be processed: in order to reduce the need for further significant capital investment in paper processing machinery; and to make room for the natural growth in paper transactions as the number of current and other account holders increases. The banks would dearly like to make inroads into the large British unbanked population, which is approximately 30% of the adult population. They are particularly hopeful that there will be an accelerated move towards 'cashless pay' (2), and that this will net them a significant increase in current account holders.

In the light of the mounting costs, the UK banks have responded by introducing cheque truncation and considering the cost reducing potential of Electronic Funds Transfer (EFT). The attractiveness of EFT will depend, in part, on the cost effectiveness of truncation. In European countries, with well developed postal Giro systems, payments can often be made more cheaply using the Giro system rather than cheques. Hence, the incentive to develop EFT may be less. As far as UK banks are concerned, the speed at which EFT is introduced will be conditioned, among other things, by its cost effectiveness.

EFT involves the transfer of money, between accounts, in response to electronically received instructions. The UK started on the road towards an EFT based system in 1968, when the Bankers Automated Clearing Services (BACS) were introduced. BACS provided for paperless clearing between the members of the Bankers Clearing House Committee (BCHC). BACS was owned by five of the six London Clearing Banks, and all six own the Bankers Clearing House (BCH), which was responsible for paper-based cheque clearing. A number of banks had direct access to cheque-based and automated clearing through membership of the BCHC. Non-member banks (i.e. non-clearing banks) had to employ one of the clearing banks as agents, in order to use the clearing system (3). In 1984 the Clearing House Automated Payments System (CHAPS), which allows same day clearing, was introduced, to improve the 'town clearing' services which apply to commercial business involving cheques of a high value. It is the general cheque clearing activity, involving private customers' cheques, that is generating the vast amounts of paper and provoking efforts to reduce costs, initially via 'truncation'. The logical next step, in the development of EFT, is to provide for automated payments involving sums smaller than those dealt with by CHAPS, between customers and retailers at the point of sale (i.e. EFTPOS). Further, the development, since 1977, of SWIFT (the Society for World Interbank Financial Telecommunication) has provided various methods of making international payments to both personal and corporate customers.

Cheque payment in the UK commonly involves a cheque, written on the account of a bank customer A, made out to a customer B, of another bank. Customer B presents the cheque to his/her bank, perhaps via another bank, and customer B's bank then sends the cheque to A's bank and, on receipt and following processing, B's account is credited and A's debited. This process is laborious and costly. 'Cheque truncation' abolishes the transfer of cheques between banks. Messages concerning transfers are instead transmitted electronically, saving significantly on costs. A drawback is that signatures cannot easily be checked, and they are currently the only legal guarantee of authorisation of funds transfer. 'Truncation', therefore, involves increased risk of fraudulent use of cheques and raises various legal questions.

EFTPOS is expected to reduce the costs of FT, beyond that achievable via 'truncation', and also to reduce the risks concerned with authorisation inherent in 'truncation'. EFTPOS will, however, raise a number of its own legal questions. Authorisation, under EFTPOS, will involve two processes. Firstly, verification that the purchaser is not impersonating somebody else when making the transactions, thus protecting the bank and the account holder from loss; and secondly, verification that the purchaser has the money or credit to make the purchase, thus protecting the bank and to some extent the retailer. The latter part of the authorisation procedure will be facilitated by an 'on-line' link between the retailer's 'checkout' and the account holder's bank. The former part will involve an identification procedure, activated by the purchaser. Currently, PINs (Personal Identification Numbers) are used to gain access to the services of Automated Teller Machines (ATMs). The PINs are punched out on the ATM, after the insertion of the debit card, in order to identify the customer and to gain authorisation for the required cash withdrawal and access to any other services provided. A similar system can be used with EFTPOS. There are, however, risks involved in PIN authorisation, since anyone can gain authorisation provided they can get hold of both the debit card and the PIN. The latter could be learnt by observation or gained through theft, if, as is commonly done, the owner has written it down. Alternative identification systems, such as electronically readable signatures, thumb prints, or photographs perhaps, might ultimately have to be considered, in order to reduce the risk of authorising unlawful usage. These would, however, be more costly to operate.

In order for EFTPOS to develop, consumers must be convinced of its merits. Once this has been done, retailers can be expected to support the development wholeheartedly; particularly because it complements their own attempts to speed up the 'checkout' procedure by introducing printed bar codes on the packaging of goods. The bar codes can be 'read' by laser scanners, to give the price of the goods, and the automated tills will total the prices of the goods in the basket and provide a printed till slip. Consumer surveys, such as those commissioned by the National Consumer Council (4) (NCC), indicate that consumers are not averse to the electronic banking services that have recently been introduced into retail banking. ATMs, for cash dispensing, have proved particularly popular because they remove some of the restrictions imposed by banking hours. ATMs are being developed to offer a much wider range of banking services, including facilities for PFT and deposit taking, and eventually they may link into EFTPOS networks. EFTPOS experiments, particularly those carried out at petrol stations in some parts of the country, have also proved popular, especially where they have provided for cash dispensing. This can be achieved by allowing customers to debit amounts in excess of their purchases. Consumers have, however, shown some reservations about 'home banking' and a move to 'plastic money' in general. One can speculate that consumers' acceptance and adoption of EFTPOS will depend: on the costs they will incur and the benefits they will derive from its introduction; on the assurances they can be given that retailers, or anyone else, will not gain access to information contained in the operations of their accounts; and on the protection consumers can be afforded from 'mistakes'. Legislation, beyond the Data Protection Act of 1985, concerning the protection of information may be needed to ensure that banks can and do preserve confidentiality and to protect consumers against the consequences of 'mistakes' (5). It is worth noting, however, that in order to obtain charge cards, especially from retailers, consumers often prove willing to supply plentiful information. In order to protect the consumer from 'mistakes' an independent record of transactions may be required. This could be achieved through the introduction of the 'smart' or 'chip' card; which has been developed in France and contains a 'microchip' capable of storing a large quantity of information, including that pertaining to recent transactions.

The extent to which the consumer will have to pay for EFTPOS depends in turn on the proportions of the costs borne by retailers and banks. It seems reasonable that costs should be borne in proportions to benefits derived, as the NCC has argued (6). The sharing of the costs of EFTPOS will be discussed further in Section 3.3.

3.2 Developing EFTPOS in the UK

In January 1985, the CLCB (7), together with the major credit card companies and with the support of some of the countries major retailers, renewed its commitment to the development of a nationwide cashless shopping system. They announced their intention to work towards a national EFTPOS system which would accept every suitable credit, cash and debit card at uniform terminals and relay the messages to the card issuers. The system is likely to use British Telecom's national communications network and IBM software and computing equipment and be capable of both on-line and off-line transactions. Current telephone charges are judged by the banks to be too expensive to allow the development of a fully on-line system. An off-line system is cheaper because information is stored for transmission to the computer centre in a 'batch' for processing after office and shopping hours. The banks want to encourage the practice of using on-line facilities only for transactions involving large, say above £20, sums of money. A decision on the limit will be a matter for negotiation between retailers and banks, but the banks could introduce higher charges for retailers requesting smaller limits.

The checkout terminals are likely to be 'sponsored' by a bank which is a member of the clearing company, see Section 2.2, Part vii. The bank will then probably accept responsibility for transactions made through its sponsored terminals. A family of terminals is envisaged to accommodate retailers who have already installed EFTPOS equipment. Some will offer only basic functions, others will be more sophisticated and add-on equipment is also likely to be provided. The cost of the terminals will vary according to their sophistication and the more basic ones may cost only a few hundred pounds. Although the system envisaged will be capable of accepting all recognised credit and debit cards, some banks are wary of allowing building societies to share the network. Some of the societies, see below, are well advanced in the development of their own electronic transmission networks. The development of the CLCB's system is being overseen by the EFTPOS Development Group under the auspices of the newly formed Payments Clearing

Services, which is sponsoring the experiments involving different types of retailers and systems.

One of the experiments was started by Midland Bank, in Autumn 1985, in Milton Keynes. It involves a mixture of retail stores and garages. It is targeted on holders of Midland and NatWest ATM cash cards and uses the same PINs. Another originates from NatWest and involves petrol stations in the Reading and Sheffield areas. It is primarily aimed at Midland and NatWest ATM cardholders but will also accept Visa and Access cards. The third, and largest, is operated by Barclaycard and will accept both Visa and Access credit cards and Amex and Diners Club charge cards. It will eliminate the currently used carbon backed paper voucher system. Customers simply sign vouchers produced by terminals and information relating to the transaction is stored and relayed electronically. It is called the Data Capture and Authorisation Retail Transactions Service (DARTS) and is concentrated largely at the Brent Cross shopping centre in N.W. London. By mid 1986 Barclaycard hoped to have 1000 terminals installed. Initial reactions from retailers was positive and a further expansion is envisaged. DARTS will rely on signature verification, rather than PINs, and will involve the transmission of transaction details, by telephone, to the Barclaycard computer after working hours.

The aim of the experiments is to accumulate information relating to the equipment, systems and consumer and retailer reactions. Other EFTPOS experiments have been operating since the early 1980s. The first was Counterplus, a joint venture between B.P. Oil and Clydesdale Bank, which began in two filling stations in Aberdeen in 1982. It proved popular with both retailers and consumers and provided additional facilities for cash withdrawals. It was extended beyond the trial period to become permanent. In October 1985, Anglia became the first building society to launch an EFTPOS scheme. It launched the first large scale cashless shopping experiment, involving over 100 retailers in Northampton. The scheme, called Paypoint, is a joint venture between Anglia and ICL, the computer manufacturer. Additionally, in August 1985, British Telecom launched a service for the electronic credit card transactions called Teletron. It clearly rivals the NatWest and Barclaycard schemes.

Meanwhile the major retailers have been considering the development of their own in-house systems. Marks and Spencer has for example introduced a transactions authorisation system based on the electronic reading of information from the M&S Chargecards, which it started to issue in 1985, and other large retailers, such as the Burton Group and those issuing the Sears Roebuck Chargecard, could follow suit. The major petrol companies could also develop their own systems. B.P., for example, has already announced the first nationwide EFTPOS system, which will ultimately operate at 2000 B.P. garages. It is to be operated with several building societies and two American banks, any of whose cards will be accepted, rather than the major clearing banks. Other major oil companies are also experimenting with EFTPOS systems at their garages. The larger retailers will ultimately have to decide whether they wish to accept a wider range of cards, and credit cards in particular, or confine their system to the chargecards they sponsor. This will in turn be conditioned by their desire to develop their own financial services divisions. Many of them, such as Tesco's and the Co-op, already offer cheque cashing facilities. These can be provided through checkouts or in-house banking offices. Others, such as Sainsbury's, allow ATMs to be situated on their premises. The major department stores have a history of providing in-house banking services, although Lewis's Bank was taken over by Lloyds in the 1980s. Sears Roebuck, in the US, has actively developed a range of retail financial services, including insurance, stock broking and banking, which it offers through its stores. Some major UK retailers seem set to follow suit. The British Home Stores has, for example, introduced BHS Boston Money Service Centres into some of its stores.

Additionally, it seems that other banks, some of them clearers but not members of the CLSB, and financial institutions, especially building societies, are not willing to allow the major clearing banks to assume the dominant position in EFTPOS that they have enjoyed in paper based clearing. This was demonstrated by the launching of LINK, also in January 1985, which is to develop a network of ATMs shared by a group of twenty-one banks and building societies. The network has been designed to have the potential for development into an EFTPOS system. The leading partners in LINK are: the Abbey National Building Society; the Co-operative Bank; the National Girobank; the Nationwide Building Society; and Funds Transfer Services (FTS). FTS is a company owned by seventeen UK and foreign institutions active in the retail financial sector, including a number of smaller building societies and American Express and

Citibank. In February 1986, another shared network of ATMs, called Matrix, was launched by seven of the UK's top building societies. The participants are the Anglia, Leeds Permanent, Bradford and Bingley, Woolwich Equitable, Leicester, National and Provincial and Alliance building societies. Each society will issue its own cards, as will the participants in LINK, and operate its own proprietry ATM system. Member's systems will be interconnected in Matrix using the IBM's value added network (VAN) service and central switch, which will control the network and provide settlement facilities. Matrix was set up by Electronic Funds Transfer, which was established in October 1983, under the auspices of the Building Societies Association, to construct a shared ATM network for building societies. Plans are also being formulated to extend the system into other financial services, including EFTPOS, where the IBM VAN switch will provide the central clearing.

Halifax, the largest UK building society, decided to introduce its own 'Cardcash' system in 1985 and rapid growth of this ATM network is planned. Thus all the major building societies are actively participating in the development of ATM networks, either individually, in the case of Halifax, or through participation in the Matrix or the LINK shared networks. Further, those involved in the shared networks are actively considering the development of their systems to provide EFTPOS services.

There is, therefore, a real risk that rival EFTPOS systems could be introduced. Not only would this be inconvenient to consumers, who would have to carry a wallet full of cards, but, because of the economies of scale involved, it would be likely to result in reduced efficiency and increased cost, in the form of charges, to the consumer. At the moment PINs and electronically readable signatures are being considered as authorisation devices. Alternative, or supplementary, techniques might have to be considered in the future, if these prove too easy to replicate by unlawful users. Additionally, users may be happier with an assurance that a record of their various transactions is being kept, independent from the computer system given the possibility of its failure and its potential for 'mistakes', and in addition to printed receipts received from checkout tills and ATMs. Towards this end the 'smart' card, developed in France and increasingly popular in the US and Japan, may have to be introduced.

3.3 **Who Should Pay For EFTPOS?**

To pursue the principle, suggested by the NCC, that costs should be borne in relation to benefits derived, it is first necessary to identify the benefits likely to be derived by the consumers, retailers and banks.

The banks' benefits will result from the cost reduction afforded by moving from PFT (Paper Funds Transfer) to EFT. Cost reductions may not, however, be immediately realised because, due to the significant economies of scale likely to be involved, the full cost reducing potential of EFT will not be achieved until the system is heavily used. Because the transfer from PFT to EFT is likely to be gradual it may take a long time for the economies to be realised. In order to maximise economies by approaching the minimum efficient scale, in a country the size of the UK, only one EFTPOS network is probably required. This has been acknowledged by the Committee of London and Scottish Bankers (CLSB), who have agreed to set up a joint EFTPOS system. A similar conclusion was reached in France, where, under the guidance of the bank supervisory authorities, the Visa and Mastercard affiliated banking groups, along with the co-operative and savings banking groups, have agreed to develop a single nationwide cashless shopping system. In the UK, however, the possibility of a number of competing networks remains, as noted in the previous section. By setting up competing systems, the consortia may eventually force the clearing banks to consider the development of a broader based EFTPOS system.

The Child Report, discussed in Section 2.2, indicated that the clearing banks would be willing, in the future, to open up access to the EFTPOS system they were developing - to non-clearing banks and building societies for example. New members would be expected to contribute to the costs of setting up the system, including research already done, however. The credible threat of the establishment of one or more competing systems would have the possible effect of reducing the entry fee and guaranteeing early access for the participants in consortia such as Matrix or LINK.

If a broadly based system eventually replaces PFT, the clearing banks' current dominant position in the provision of FT services would be lost. The opportunities for economies of scale in the provision of EFT services suggest that they could be provided by a 'natural monopoly' (8). If this is indeed the case, then one might ask whether EFT should instead be developed under the guidance of the Bank of England. Once established, it could be run by a government agency or a private company, perhaps outside the banking system. Given the public utility or infrastructural status of the payments system, which is not unlike that of the telecommunications system through which it will probably function, the question of whether it is best operated in the public or the private sector arises. Arguments pertaining to the 'privatisation' of British Telecom in the early 1980s then become germane. A guiding role for the Bank would be in keeping with its responsibility for overseeing the efficient development of the banking system, in general, and the payments system, in particular.

It is worth stressing that the 'set up' costs of EFTPOS are likely to be high. The hardware involved, such as the computers and the sales terminals, will itself be costly, but it is the software, the operating programs, etc., and the arrangements to prevent unlawful access and fraud that are proving to be increasingly costly.

The retailers stand to gain, if the consumers take to the system, and may indeed be forced to adopt it to retain consumer patronage. If EFTPOS reduced checkout queues significantly, it may well attract additional customers. Retailers may also gain through a reduction in the credit 'float' extended to customers under the current PFT system. The 'float' arises out of the time it takes for cheques to clear under the PFT system. EFT, with 'on-line' account adjustments, can eliminate the 'float' and also reduce risks of non-payment. If EFT is developed to permit consumers to withdraw cash, as well as to pay the shopping bill, then retailers can also gain favour by enhancing their role as cash dispensers. Alternatively, they could allow ATMs to be made available in shops and reduce the necessary amount of cash held in tills.

Consumers should be attracted to the system, provided that information dissemination, fraud and other (9) fears can be abated, if EFT does in fact reduce the cost of FT relative to PFT, and also if it reduces checkout queues and saves on the time involved in using credit cards. A major problem is presented by the fact that consumers are not accustomed to paying for the full cost of PFT services. Until recently, some charges were made by most banks but these only covered a proportion of the costs of providing the services. Even when customers are offered the advantage of 'free banking' services

(10), however, they commonly make an implicit payment through non-receipt of interest on current account balances. The practice of not paying interest on current account balances affords the banks an 'endowment effect', which varies with the rate of interest earned on lending and usually provides them with a clear profit, after deducting an implicit interest rate reflecting non-recovered costs. This system of charges has the effect that infrequent cheque users who hold large current account balances subsidise frequent cheque users with low current account balances. A more economically efficient system would charge fully for the PFT services used and would attract current account depositors by paying interest on positive balances. Compared with such a system of charges for PFT, the cost advantages of EFT would be clear to the consumer and it would probably be welcomed with open arms. Prior to 1985, the major clearing banks paid implicit interest on current accounts, largely regardless of the balance held provided it exceeded a stated minimum, by not making full charges for usage of the PFT system and hoped to attract current account deposits in this way. This charging system carries the advantage for the consumer that the implicit interest is not subject to taxation, composite or otherwise. 'Free banking', with no charges provided a positive balance is held in the account and no interest, proved extremely popular, however, and banks offering this service were gaining customers at the expense of banks which required minimum balances and made at least some charges. It was not clear, however, from the NCC commissioned surveys (11) that the consumers perceived the prevailing system of bank charges, with no interest on current account balances, and implicit cross subsidisation of heavy cheque users by less frequent cheque users, as advantageous to them. In 1985, the major clearing banks, following the Midland Bank which had introduced 'free banking' in 1984, all decided to offer 'free banking' to customers maintaining positive balances and the previous non-zero credit balance requirements were dropped. This was a response to growing competition, from the Midland Bank, smaller clearing banks and building societies, for retail banking business. Punitive charges, which vary considerably between banks, are imposed for a period of up to three months, on customers whose balances fall below zero. In addition, most banks introduced interest bearing cheque accounts, for which some customers could qualify, alongside their standard current accounts.

This was also a response to competition from other financial institutions, especially building societies, which were introducing interest bearing accounts which provided a significant subset of the services made available through standard bank current accounts.

The problem faced by the banks is that a move to an economically efficient charging system would require a significant rise in the level of bank charges. Some of these charges would be needed to cover the costs involved in the distribution of notes and coins, which are issued by the Bank and the Royal Mint respectively. These costs, of distributing the legal tender, fall largely on banks and their customers and yet the non-banked and those gaining access to banking services via building societies and other non-bank financial institutions do not contribute fully to the costs of cash distribution. Thus bank customers are cross subsidising the dominant and major alternative, non-PFT and non-EFT, payments system. A more equitable system would meet the costs of cash distribution out of taxation and reduce bank charges at a stroke, as the NCC has observed (12). Given the Bank of England's ultimate responsibility, subect to its accountability to the Treasury, for the payments and banking systems, and the fact that it is an issuer of legal tender and has responsibility for cash distribution, it might be appropriate for the Bank to take prime responsibility for cash distribution and to receive the necessary funds to perform the task from the Treasury.

The present charging system for PFT will probably make the rapid introduction of EFT much more difficult. This is because it will be more difficult for consumers to perceive the cost advantages of EFT and also because banks may consequently have to absorb not only some of the 'set up' costs but also some of the running costs, some of which the consumer might be expected to bear. Clearly the banks should adopt a long run perspective, in order to encourage the use of the EFT system so that economies of scale can be reaped and barriers to entry erected. The proportion of the costs they must absorb is, however, likely to be greater as a result of the present PFT charging system. Various solutions to this problem are open to the banks. They could offer EFT services 'free' and rely on the interest earned on EFT account balances to cover the costs. They could introduce an economically rational charging system, for both EFT and PFT services, combined with interest rate payments on current account balances. This would encourage the use of EFTPOS if payments could be made more cheaply than by cheque. Alternatively, they could pay higher interest on special EFT accounts than on normal cheque book based current accounts. They could also combine lower charges for EFT accounts with higher interest.

Given that consumers stand to lose their three day credit float from retailers, higher interest could be offered in recompense on EFT current accounts. Alternatively, small credit facilities could be made available, to compensate. The float could be maintained initially, if its loss is expected to reduce the popularity of EFTPOS. This could be done by introducing an EFTPOS system with 'on-line' authorisation but delayed payments, which is the system most likely to be developed, see Section 3.2. This would allow 'batch' submissions to banks, requesting payment for perhaps a whole day's worth of consumers' purchases, which would reduce the cost of EFT compared with a fully 'on-line' system. The retailers could postdate their requests for payment to maintain the float. It is likely, however, that retailers will want to reduce the float in order to reduce their own needs for credit and, therefore, their costs. It is not obvious anyway that the consumer values the credit advantages, afforded by the two to three day cheque clearing period, very highly. This may be because the standard current account credit balances bear no interest and it is only really end of month payments that reap the benefit of the time lag involved in cheque payments. If it proved necessary, the combination of EFT accounts with small overdraft facilities could offset the loss of the float. Some consumers have anyway proved willing to give up the credit advantages of cheque usage by using ATMs, which effect same day account debiting, in order to get cash. A conflicting trend has been the increasing interest, shown by consumers of retail banking services, in interest bearing accounts that offer many of the basic current account services. The growing sophistication of consumers of retail financial services may eventually lead interest bearing current accounts to become the norm. Such a development will become more likely when building societies start to offer cheque guarantee cards, making their interest bearing cheque accounts even more attractive, and unsecured loans, enabling them to attract new business and cross sell other services. They were permitted to offer these and other services by the 1986 Building Society Act (13) and the result will be a significant increase in their ability to compete with banks in the retail financial services market. It is, therefore, not clear what value consumers currently place on the float, inherent in cheque payment, but their valuation of it may increase as interest bearing cheque accounts become more widely available.

Consumers should really only be expected to cover the cost of moving money from their account to a retailer's. They are unlikely to be willing to pay more, since their increasing access to ATM facilities, as the various networks expand apace, provides them with access to a relatively cheap alternative means of payment, i.e. cash.

Retailers should expect to pay for the advantage of a reduced float, if the reduction proves acceptable to consumers, which will lead to a corresponding fall in their own credit needs. To the extent that EFTPOS nets extra sales and reduces risks involved in transactions, they might also expect to pay some commission. The improvements in the authorisation system, which are likely to be afforded by EFT, would appear to benefit retailers and banks jointly and they should, therefore, expect to share in the costs of installing the necessary equipment at checkouts.

Banks should expect to have to subsidise services, until significant economies of scale can be achieved, but will receive partially offsetting commissions from retailers, and perhaps consumers, and savings due to the rundown of PFT and the possible reduction of fraud risks.

Agreement on the sharing of 'set up' costs, between banks and retailers, has proved difficult to achieve in most of the countries introducing or experimenting with such systems (14). Until agreement is reached, however, the widespread introduction of EFTPOS will be stalled. Final agreement will clearly depend on perceived costs and benefits and bargaining power. The extent to which consumers should be expected to contribute directly to 'set up' costs, through charges, is debatable. If the system's development is in the interests of the whole economy, then the option remains to be considered of state subsidisation, perhaps via a loan, of 'set up' costs, out of tax revenue and, therefore, for the consumers to pay indirectly. If the EFT system is to remain in the private sector, it might make sense for the government to provide the subsidy in return for future commission, unless the subsidy takes the form of an interest bearing loan.

To conclude the discussion on who should pay for EFTPOS, we can note that ultimately the consumer should expect to pay for the funds transfer services used, allowing the banks some profit, and the retailers and banks for the authorisation and computer hardware equipment and the software needed to establish the system. It is after all the banks that are in the business of financial intermediation and the retailers who are in the business of selling goods to the consumer. They should, therefore, expect to have to make the capital investment necessary to undertake the business efficiently.

The pace of EFT introduction depends largely on how quickly agreement can be reached and the appropriate sharing of costs. The system must first be sold to the consumers and the present charging system for PFT militates against this. The problems concerning: protection of information; the legality and acceptability of authorisation procedures; and protecting the system from 'mistakes' and potentially massive frauds, must be dealt with. This will require, in part, sophisticated software and extensive and costly policing of the system, and probably relatively expensive authorisation devices, such as the 'chip' or 'smart' card. Widespread usage of EFTPOS, and especially the fully electronic 'cashless' banking system that might develop out of it, is probably at least a decade away.

The ultimate development could be the elimination of bank branch networks, ATMs, and retail outlets, with all banking transactions taking place via a computer link from the home to banks and retailers' catalogues. The cashless and shopless society would then have arrived. The NCC commissioned surveys (15) indicates that this will not be readily accepted in the near future. People not only like to see the goods that they are to buy with their hard earned incomes, but they like the personal touch in arranging various banking transactions. One might, however, speculate that the 'cashless society' is more likely to occur than the shopless one.

3.4 Conclusions

EFT provides an opportunity for increasing the efficiency of the payments system, in the sense of providing for faster transfers at lower cost and, perhaps, with reduced risk. The future development of the electronic payments system gives some cause for concern, however. We noted that the Wilson Report had stated that, if we were starting anew, a publicly owned clearing system might be an attractive proposition. We are in fact virtually starting anew with this system, although it should be recognised that the major clearing banks have already incurred some costs in preparing the groundwork for the system. Whilst public ownership is probably unnecessary there does seem to be a case here for some direct public involvement, perhaps via the Bank of England, in the development of a nationwide cashless shopping system with wide membership and coverage. This would be in keeping with the Bank's responsibility for ensuring that an efficient payments system is in operation and with the Child Report's recommendations, which gives the Bank more effective supervisory powers over the clearing system. This is by virtue of the requirement that members of the clearing companies must have settlement accounts with the Bank, which has not stated its criteria for judging the suitability of applicants, and that the Bank is to be a member of the umbrella organisation and the various companies, as of right. Additionally, it is to be represented on the Steering Committee, also chaired by D.M. Child, which is to implement the Child Report's recommendations as soon as possible. To facilitate the development of an efficient nationwide electronic payments system, it will be necessary to avoid overlapping networks, in order to reap the maximum reward from economies of scale.

EFTPOS's speed of introduction is likely to be hindered by a number of obstacles, the primary one being the allocation of costs between retailers, banks and consumers. There is an opportunity here, and perhaps an obligation, for the monetary authorities to smooth the path, and possibly even to take the lead, given the infrastructural characteristics of the FT system. This could be done, with minimum governmental intervention, by no longer requiring banks and their customers to shoulder the bulk of the cost of cash distribution and by subsidising EFT introduction until economies of scale can be realised. In return, the authorities might require that access to the national EFT system would be completely open to banks and non-banks, particularly building societies and non-clearing banks, alike. The major banks should have no objection to this provided that state sponsorship is sufficient to allow them to recoup some or all of the capital they have already sunk into the development of EFTPOS systems. Taxes would have to rise a bit to cover the costs incurred by the monetary authorities, perhaps by introducing a special rate of VAT on bank service charges. The introduction of a more efficient and more equitably funded monetary transactions system would be the prize. If, in addition, interest is paid on current account credit balances, in the EFT system, and there is full charging for services used, then tax revenue would be increased. Hence taxes may not have to rise by much, if at all, to fund the subsidised introduction of EFT.

EFT offers the gateway to a fully electronic banking system and if this develops alongside deregulation then the efficiency of financial intermediation should improve significantly and we may even be able to do without money as we know it.

It has been suggested that, in a fully deregulated financial system, the distinction between bank and non-bank financial intermediaries would disappear (16). The current special status of banks is the result of regulations, imposed by monetary authorities, which have the effect that banks are the only institutions whose liabilites are money and that they are restricted, by reserve requirements and other controls, to lending below profit maximising levels. In a deregulated system, all financial intermediaries would be able to engage in EFT. If they all eventually offered EFT services, because competition had forced banks to offer portfolio management services and non-bank financial intermediaries to provide monetary transmission services, broker-banking institutions (BBIs) would emerge. The financial system in such a world might well consist of a number of interlinking accounts and EFT would involve sending electronic instructions to debit one account and credit another somewhere in the system. The volume of liabilities in the system would accord with consumer preferences and would not be restricted by a reserve ratio imposed by the monetary authorities. BBIs' profits would depend on the cost of attracting funds and the charges made for the loan, brokerage and payment services provided. BBIs would maintain a system of accounts and provide brokerage services for consumers. EFT would not require the existence of a physical means of payment or even the concept of money. Initially, BBIs would hold portfolios of assets and EFT would involve monetary transactions requiring portfolio adjustment by the BBIs. Ultimately, money might not be required, since banks would offer accounts with varying degrees of risk and commensurate return and EFT would permit transfers from any one account to any other, thereby facilitating portfolio adjustment. Since BBIs would merely respond to customers' risk or portfolio preferences, they would have no independent influence on the economic allocation of funds through their portfolio management activities.

In such a world it becomes clear that there is no compelling reason why provision of transfer services should be undertaken solely by financial institutions, which would just need to link into the system in order to provide bookkeeping and portfolio management services. There is, as mentioned above, something infrastructural about the FT system of an economy.

Issues such as: whether money will ever be completely eliminated in the financial system; whether cash or legal tender will ever command interest payments; whether the numeraire will be a commodity; and whether the government will relinquish its monopoly over the supply of legal tender; are just a few examples of opportunities for financial economic science fiction analysis. There is in fact a burgeoning literature on alternative monetary and financial constitutions and systems (17).

Notes

1. See Inter-Bank Research Organisation (1982) for further details.

2. I.e. payments of wages and salaries directly into bank or building society accounts rather than in the form of 'wage packets'.

3. These arrangements are likely to change following the Child Report, see Section 2.2, Part iv.

4. See National Consumer Council (1983, Appendices II and III).

5. There is little legislation giving consumers protection when computers, or their controllers, make 'mistakes', see Goode (1985) for further discussion.

6. See National Consumer Council (1983).

7. Since then the CLSB has replaced the CLCB, see note 47, Chapter 2.

8. See Section 2.2, Part viii.

9. Especially concerning mistaken transactions and mistaken confiscation of cards by ATMs.

10. See below.

11. See note 4.

12. See note 6.

13. See Section 4.2

14. See The Banker (1986) for a review of progress in the development of various EFTPOS schemes in operation worldwide. Hong Kong's 'Easy Pay' system has proved to be an exception, with its rapid introduction and wide acceptance, see Haney (1985) for a more detailed discussion of electronic banking in Hong Kong.

15. See note 4.

16. See for example Tobin (1963), Black (1970) and Fama (1980).

17. See for example Journal of Monetary Economics (1983), Vol. 12, which contains a number of articles discussing such issues.

Chapter Four

UK FINANCIAL DEREGULATION IN THE 1980s

4.1 Introduction

The deregulation of the UK financial system in the 1980s has taken place in the context of the growing globalisation of financial markets and worldwide deregulation. UK deregulation has both responded to these developments and been a causal factor, especially with regard to European deregulation in the capital markets.

As noted in Chapter 2, traditional demarcations in the UK banking system began to break down in the 1970s. Not only did this process accelerate in the 1980s but traditional demarcations between the banking and the wider financial system also began to crumble. The 1970s also witnessed an internationalisation of banking (1) and increasing competition from foreign banks which had established themselves in London, either directly or through consortium banks (2). Also in the 1970s, the Eurobond market grew significantly and international trading in the securities of major multinational companies developed. The prospect of globalised securities markets with twenty-four hour trading, revolving around major financial centres in the various time zones, became increasingly realistic. The UK stock market remained aloof from these developments even though London was host to the Euromarkets. It was a closed shop with a trading system which was out of line with the practices of the markets in other major financial centres, such as Tokyo and New York.

The removal of foreign exchange controls in October 1979 was the first major deregulatory measure introduced by the Thatcher government. It was followed by a major build up of foreign shares in the portfolios of insurance and pension funds and increased awareness of the possibilities for international securities trading. The government and the UK monetary authorities, particularly the Bank of England, realised that the City could potentially dominate the European time zone, opening the way for twenty-four hour global securities trading, revolving around the London, Tokyo and New York stock exchanges, in line with similar developments in the foreign exchange markets.

Twenty-four hour trading in the foreign exchange markets, revolving around Tokyo, London and New York, is a virtual reality. Surveys were conducted simultaneously by the central banks of the UK, the US and Japan in 1986. In 1985, the Group of Thirty (3) had published a study indicating that foreign exchange turnover amounted to $150 bn a day. Some commentators thought this to be a gross overestimate but the central banks found that the daily turnover in the three major centres was $188 bn. The New York Federal Reserve Bank estimated that turnover in New York had increased by 92% since 1983. The market is, therefore, large and has been growing very rapidly. The world market has so far been dominated by trading between the Deutsche-Mark (D. Mark) and the dollar, although sterling/dollar trading is most important in London and D.Mark/sterling trading has been increasing rapidly. The three major centres are taking a growing share of the world market and the largest banks are becoming increasingly dominant. In London the major players are the big clearers and some of the major US banks. The business in London took off after the lifting of exchange controls in 1979. This permitted banks to trade currencies with each other directly, rather than through brokers. The foreign exchange brokers still do a healthy business, arranging 43% of the business in a vastly expanded market. The Bank of England's survey, carried out in March 1986, shows the average daily turnover in London to be $90 bn, nearly double accepted estimates. This put the London market ahead of the New York and Tokyo markets, which had estimated turnovers of $50 bn and $48 bn respectively.

By 1983 the Office of Fair Trading (OFT) had built up a case against the Stock Exchange and sought permission from the Department of Trade and Industry to take it to the Restrictive Practices Court. Instead a deal was struck in 1983, between the Secretary of State for Industry and the Chairman of the Stock Exchange, to end the practice of setting minimum commissions. It was hoped that this would increase the Exchange's international competitiveness. This deal combined with the removal of exchange controls led to a build up of pressure for a more substantial reform of the Exchange culminating in the Big Bang, on 27 October 1986. These developments were not only a reponse to international pressures but generated their own pressures for the deregulation of other major European capital markets. Other European countries engaged in what was effectively competitive deregulation, designed to maintain the status of established financial centres such as Amsterdam, Frankfurt and Paris in the face of the growing threat that London might eventually dominate the European time zone (4).

Whilst the Stock Exchange was preparing for the Big Bang there was, however, an accelerated growth of the Eurobond markets. The Mexican Crisis in 1982 (5) had discouraged further growth in the syndicated loan market and caused the major UK clearing banks to reassess their strategies with regard to international and domestic business development. They decided to build up their retail banking business, which had been somewhat neglected in the 1970s allowing building societies and smaller banks to make major inroads, and to securitise their international business. The Euronote market, for example, grew rapidly in the first half of the 1980s (6). The success of this securitisation has also encouraged banks to consider opportunities for securitisation in the domestic market, see Section 4.4. The securitisation process, which has continued as banks have attempted to fight off competition to meet the needs of their major corporate and government clients, has led banks to become increasingly involved in capital markets and accelerated the breakdown of traditional demarcations between bank and non-bank financial intermediaries. Securitisation has major implications for both the banks and the Stock Exchange. By 1986 the Eurobond market, which incorporates the Euronote market, had become London's largest securities market and was as important a source of finance for the industrial and commercial companies as either the Stock Exchange or the bank credit market. It is a market dominanted by the world's major Japanese and US securities houses, which are jointly represented by the Association of International Bond Dealers (AIBD). The Stock Exchange Council (SEC) had assumed that the reform of market practices it was encouraging would leave the Stock Exchange well placed to expand into the international arena. The international securities dealers were, however, at the same time developing their trade in big name equities and were poised to poach a large slice of the market. It, therefore, became evident that the reform of the Stock Echange might have come too late. Not only were the major companies able to raise long and medium term funds on the Eurobond markets but they were increasingly exploiting opportunities to raise short term, working capital, funds on the growing Euro-commercial paper market. They were, therefore, increasingly able to bypass not only the Stock Exchange but also the banks. The banks have consequently been losing some of their traditional blue chip corporate lending business and been forced to concentrate on developing loan business in the middle corporate market and the personal sector. In addition they have moved into merchant and investment banking in order to increase fee income, to replace their lost earnings from lending, and to follow their major corporate customers in order to retain their custom for remunerative non-lending services.

In line with the government's policy of freeing markets, to allow them to operate more flexibly and efficiently, other deregulatory measures have been introduced in the 1980s. These measures have been designed to increase competition, especially in the retail banking sector, and involve the removal of restrictions and distortions. By increasing competition they added impetus to the developments in the 1970s, discussed in Chapter 2. Tax changes have been used both to encourage activity in the financial markets and to remove distortions. In the 1984 Budget, for example, it was announced: that the Composite Rate of Taxation (CRT) imposed on building societies was to be extended to banks; that Life Assurance Premium Relief was to be abolished, removing a bias towards savings through insurance; that stamp duty would be halved to 1%, to encourage stock market turnover and small shareholding; and that there would be a phased reduction in capital allowances and taxes were consequently liable on banks' leasing business. Apart from the reduction in stamp duty, which was further halved in the 1986 Budget, the government has introduced a number of measures in pursuit of its goal of achieving wider share ownership. These have included: the abolition of the investment income surcharge; the reduction and modification of capital gains tax; the introduction of the Business Expansion Scheme; and the proposals for encouraging the development of Personal Equity Plans and Profit Related Pay announced in the 1986 Budget. These measures have been complemented by the government's privatisation programme, which itself has contained measures encouraging wide ownership of floated shares. Other objectives behind the government's desire to promote efficiency in the City have been: to create a better market for gilts to make funding easier and cheaper; and to ensure that the City continues to contribute to the UK's traditional invisible trade surplus (7).

The Bank of England, which has collaborated closely with the SEC over the Exchange's reform, because of its interest in the gilts market by virtue of its responsibility for managing the government's funding programme, has been keen to promote London as an international financial centre. The participants have, in the main, been keen to win more international business and the major banks have become eager to gain a share of the gilts market.

The remainder of this chapter is organised as follows. The build up to the Big Bang will first be outlined. This will be followed by a discussion of other deregulatory measures involving the retail banking sector and especially the building societies and the Trustee Savings Banks. It will conclude with a review of other developments in the financial markets and a discussion of the possible implications of the deregulation in the post Big Bang period.

4.2 The Big Bang

The Big Bang is not an unpremeditated explosion, but the result of careful planning and wide consultation, as the Chairman of the SEC, Sir Nicholas Goodison, has pointed out (8). On 27 October 1986 minimum commissions were abolished and a new dealing system in UK securities was introduced. It was an event in a series of improvements and is unlikely to create a new financial world overnight. It is, therefore, something of a misnomer.

The restructuring of the Stock Exchange, as Goodison prefers to call it, is the result of an evolutionary process responding to pressures exerted by the developments in the international markets and in the technologies of communications and data processing, which themselves have facilitated international developments. These developments have rendered the traditional single capacity dealing system, which has operated for over 200 years, anachronistic. The single capacity dealing system was based on a firm division of function between brokers and jobbers. Jobbers bought and sold shares on the trading floor under the instruction of brokers; they did not deal directly with investors. Brokers acted on behalf of clients and could not deal directly on the market. Brokers, therefore, provided an agency service, advising and acting on behalf of clients, and the jobbers executed brokers' orders to buy and sell shares. Brokers earnt income by means of a fixed commission for each transaction whilst the jobbers' income was based on their 'turn', the difference between the buying and selling price.

Because of exchange controls the Stock Exchange was unable to participate in the growing international shares market during the 1960s and 1970s. Following the removal of exchange controls in 1979, a tremendous interest was shown in international markets by UK investors. The UK securities firms lacked expertise and, due to single capacity and minimum commissions, were unable to compete with the prices charged by foreign firms. Additionally, they were undercapitalised compared to the major international securities houses and, therefore, unable to participate in purchases and sales on the scale required by institutions such as the major insurance companies.

Domestic pressures for change also accumulated as a result of the growing domination of the stock market by insurance and pension funds, which increasingly wished to trade stocks and shares in blocks. These caused a rise in the average size of transactions forcing jobbing firms to merge in order to spread and pool risks and increase capitalisation (9). Any further reduction in their number would have resulted in inadequate competition. Additionally, institutional investors grew increasingly critical of minimum commissions, especially in the growing gilts market, and the number of brokers also declined significantly (10), in response to a shrinking client base and the increasing cost of providing the services demanded.

Despite these domestic and international pressures, the Stock Exchange resisted change and it took the government, in its efforts to promote a low cost dealing system and encourage private share holding, to spark the change. The OFT had completed its investigation by early 1983 and had uncovered 150 Stock Exchange rules which it believed could be challenged under the Restrictive Trade Practices Act 1976. The OFT's case, which was expected to be submitted for judgement to the Restrictive Practices Court in December 1983, concentrated on three main issues: the single capacity system of trading; fixed commissions; and restricted membership, which prohibited outsiders from having interests in excess of 29.9% in one member firm and 5% in a second. The SEC had power to grant exemption to the latter rule. On 19 July 1983 the Chairman of the SEC, Sir Nicholas Goodison, struck a deal with Cecil Parkinson, the Secretary of State for Trade and Industry. In return for the withdrawal of the OFT's case, the SEC promised to abolish fixed commissions by the end of 1986. The Bank of England was to be involved in the reform and David Walker, a director of the Bank, emerged as the behind the scenes orchestrator of much of the City's ensuing restructuring.

It soon became apparent that the ending of minimum commissions would lead to other changes. This generated some debate concerning whether the liberalisation of Stock Exchange practices should occur simultaneously and within a short space of time, literally a Big Bang, or be introduced slowly over a period. The Bank and the Stock Exchange opted for a period of consultation and preparation, in which institutions could prepare themselves and the SEC could sponsor the development of a computer based dealing system. The 27 October 1986 date was set, some three and a half years after the Goodison-Parkinson agreement and just inside the time limit. It remains a Big Bang of sorts, but much of the preparatory work had been completed by mid 1986.

Following the agreement to end fixed commissions, the SEC, under the guidance of the Bank, also decided to open the doors of the Exchange to all those willing to pay the entry fee and to abandon single capacity. These developments were opposed by many Stock Exchange members, especially the smaller ones. They were appeased somewhat by the SEC's promise to charge entry fees that would be sufficient to compensate existing members for the opening up of the market. The more altruistic members argued that single capacity should be retained because of the investor protection it inherently afforded (11). The dominant view was, however, that minimum commissions and single capacity were inextricably linked. Those adhering to the 'link theory' argued that, having agreed to abolish minimum commissions, single capacity must also go, because brokers would be unable to function except by bypassing the market and matching buying or selling orders, within their firms, forcing jobbers to seek new clients. The Bank argued that the introduction of dual capacity was necessary to bring the Stock Exchange into line with worldwide trading practices and further that, to make the market international, it was essential to open up membership to overseas securities houses.

Having decided to adopt dual capacity, the implementation of the new dealing system had to await the development of a computer based system capable of ensuring investor protection and allowing adequate policing of market practices. Also, following the decision to open the doors to the heavily capitalised overseas securities houses, it was necessary to allow increased capitalisation of domestic securities firms so that they could compete. After the Goodison-Parkinson agreement the SEC permitted a whole series of participations, often in both jobbing and broking firms, up to the maximum of 29.9%, by both domestic and overseas financial institutions. The SEC also proposed to allow participations of 100% from 1 March 1986, an earlier date being precluded because it would have impaired the functioning of the traditional system and because the monetary authorities had not developed a policy for dealing with potential bank insolvencies on the stock market. In 1983 the authorities had made it clear that banks would be a legitimate source of capital and the merger wave (12), which continued right up to the Big Bang, began. The continuing opposition from some members, to the proposal to open up membership of the exchange, was overcome in 1985, when the SEC announced that it would welcome new members, including those from overseas, with effect from 1 March 1986, even if they had not acquired existing members.

In the new, post Big Bang, dual capacity system member firms became broker-dealers. They are able to act both as agency brokers, providing advice and acting on behalf of clients, and as principals, buying and selling shares on their own account. Broker-dealers can also become market makers, who will be required to buy or sell, during business hours, stocks which they have nominated and to stand by quoted prices. To ensure that the market has the confidence of both the practitioners and the investors, the SEC has overhauled its rule book (13) and its regulation and surveillance procedures. The Bank has decided that the gilts market should remain within the Stock Exchange and has devised rules, trading and regulatory practices (14) for the market, designed to complement those of the SEC.

The Stock Exchange introduced a new electronic price information system called the Stock Exchange Automated Quotation System (SEAQ). It shows a complete list of all market makers in a particular security together with the buying and selling price they are quoting and the volume for which the prices hold. It will monitor and store all dealing information to enable the SEC to supervise the market. For investor protection it is also necessary to ensure the rapid settlement of business. For this purpose, its TALISMAN computer settlement system has been modernised and improved. Further, new rules have been drafted which are designed to prevent the conflicts of interest which might occur when a firm provides advice to an investor concerning particular shares and is concurrently dealing in them on its own behalf. Stocks and shares are graded according to their volume and turnover. Only information on α, β and δ stocks is displayed in SEAQ. The most information is displayed for α stocks and the least for δ stocks. There is a charge for plugging into SEAQ and some broker-dealers have chosen not to use it. Some market makers have continued to operate outside SEAQ, dealing over the telephone or on the floor, the life of which, many believe, is limited.

The restructuring of the Stock Exchange will not cease with the Big Bang. There are plans to introduce a computerised automatic execution system for smaller orders and the SEC is working on the development of a paperless transfer system. In May 1986, the SEC issued a paper discussing proposals for the establishment of a third market. It had introduced a second market, the Unlisted Securities Market (USM), which allows growing medium sized companies to issue shares without seeking a full stock market quotation, in 1980. The third market will deal in the shares of immature companies and facilitate the provision of venture capital. An unofficial 'over the counter' (OTC) market has grown in unlisted stocks of immature companies. It has been loosely regulated by the Department of Trade and Industry under the Prevention of Fraud (Investments) Acts. Under the investor protection legislation proposed in the Financial Services Bill (15), the OTC market would have to be supervised by a Self Regulatory Organisation (SRO) and the Securities and Investment Board (SIB) (16) would ideally like the OTC to become a Recognised Investment Exchange (RIE). Nasdim (17), which has applied for recognition from the SIB as an SRO, believed that the establishment of an RIE for the OTC market would prove too expensive. The SEC has taken the initiative by proposing a third market, access to which is to be limited to Stock Exchange member firms. Its proposal partially resolves the regulatory problems but is clearly an attempt to bring the OTC market within the Stock

Exchange, leaving a large number of participants in the OTC market out in the cold. Their response was to form a committee, representing practitioners in the OTC market, to explore the possibility of financing a rival OTC exchange called the London Securities Exchange. They hope to have it running by the end of 1986 and to apply to the SIB for it to be approved as an RIE. Fragmentation of the OTC market is, therefore, a prospect unless the SEC drops its exclusion restriction, the case for which is weak, and comes to an agreement with the OTC committee and also with Nasdim, concerning supervision of the market.

In August 1986, the SEC published another discussion document, proposing to remove most of the restrictions on issues of new shares, including the requirement to give existing shareholders first refusal on new shares issued in the main market and the USM. The proposals, following discussions and revisions, took effect from 27 October 1986 and are expected to make new issues cheaper by reducing reliance on underwriting. They were opposed by the investor protection committee of pension and insurance funds - ostensibly because they will dilute small share holdings but, being the major shareholders themselves, the funds may be more concerned about not being offered first refusal themselves. Initially, the institutional investment managers expected the ending of minimum commissions to bring them an undiluted benefit, by reducing dealing costs, because of their strong bargaining position in negotiating commissions after the Big Bang. They did not foresee that far more was at stake than the cost of transactions. Under fixed commissions, brokers had the responsibility for dealing, providing research, and installing the hardware necessary to perform these functions. After the Big Bang, fund managers will have to decide whether to hire their own dealers, to seek the best prices, and face the burden of negotiating commissions and doing some of the research themselves. Moreover, the reforms have gone much further than removing minimum commissions. Consequently, whilst the investment institutions are likely to gain more control over the cost of secondary trading through negotiated commissions, they may lose their dominant position in the new issue market to the securities firms.

Alongside the secondary market's fixed commissions scale, a similar fixed scale of sub-underwriting charges has operated in the primary market. Academic studies show this to be much higher than justified by the risk involved. Fund managers have seemed happy with the underwriting cartel, operated by merchant banks and stock brokers active in corporate finance, and have not bid for underwriting business at cut rates. Instead, they have been happy to take on lucrative sub-underwriting business. The potential loss of sub-underwriting income may, therefore, lie behind their opposition to the SEC's new issue proposals. The cartel is already crumbling anyway. Lazard Brothers, the merchant bank, cut the sub-underwriting commission by half for the TSB flotation, discussed in Section 4.4, which it sponsored and Prudential, the insurance company, launched a deeply discounted rights issue of its own shares in 1986, to avoid underwriting. The increased competition in the post Big Bang market will severely trim the profits from secondary trading and the securities houses will probably seek to make up the difference in the primary market, causing a collapse of the underwriting cartel. Competition may not, therefore, just result in large commissions savings but is likely to have much wider ramifications. The New York Stock Exchange's experience, following its deregulation in 1975, was that the competitive pressures led to the creation of large aggressive securities houses. The investment fund managers should, therefore, prepare for such a development in the UK rather than complain about the slippage in standards.

The most exciting prospect, and the one for which reform was deemed necessary to further, is the prospect of growth in the trading of international securities. The aim has been to prepare for the provision of an efficient and liquid market in international securities that will capture a significant share of the market, especially in the European time zone. In June 1985 the Stock Exchange launched SEAQ International, an electronic market place for all the largest international securities houses, dealing in more than 600 leading equities. It is also developing links with other European, US and S.E. Asian stock exchanges and with NASDAQ, the major US OTC market and the third largest, in terms of value and turnover, stock exchange in the world. The London Stock Exchange is the fourth largest and only the New York and Tokyo stock exchanges are larger than NASDAQ. In August 1985, 11 Hong Kong shares appeared on the SEAQ Internatioanl screens, which already displayed prices for major South African and Australian shares. In total prices for 550 foreign shares were being quoted by the 35 market makers.

As noted above, within London there is already a larger securities market, the Eurobond market. It is represented by the Association of International Bond Dealers (AIBD) which, in conjunction with the IPMA (18), set up a potential SRO called Isro (19). Members of the AIBD and the IPMA had already started to diversify into international stock dealing and consequently threatened the SEC's ambition to keep the dealing in international stocks within the Stock Exchange. The fear of fragmentation forced the SEC to enter into negotiations with Isro and to lower entry charges to attract membership from international securities houses. It proved unrealistic to expect to be able to compensate existing members fully for the opening up of the market. Isro oversees a market in which only professionals participate and its members do not wish to be burdened by complex Stock Exchange rules designed to protect both investors and member firms. Isro and the Stock Exchange, however, have a common interest in capitalising on London's opportunity in the global market place. Isro was expected to be recognised by the SIB and the AIBD was considering the possibility of becoming an RIE with automated trading.

Isro and the SEC entered into negotiations in May 1986 and set up a joint working party to consider a possible merger of the two proposed SROs into a single SRO to authorise and monitor firms in all the securities markets, both domestic and international, in London. It was supposed to report by the end of July but ultimately the SEC and Isro issued joint proposals in September 1986. The most sensitive area of negotiation concerned the international equities market. The international securities houses, which had dealt primarily in the Eurobond markets in London, had increasingly been trading in major shares of all nationalities. The Stock Exchange was anxious to avoid becoming a market for small shares with the more important α stocks traded outside. Another crucial issue is the choice of screen system. The SEC favours its own SEAQ International, which displays prices of several hundred foreign shares. Isro has been considering alternatives, including that used by NASDAQ. The decision to broaden negotiations to include the study of a merger of the two bodies SRO functions followed the realisation that, given the cost of establishing effective self-regulation and the overlap in their responsibilities, because distinctions between international and domestic business were progressively breaking down, it might be efficient. The costs of establishing an effective SRO would be greatest for Isro because it would be starting from scratch, the Eurobond market being previously unregulated, and had few staff, whereas the Stock Exchange has long practised self-regulation. Additionally, the SEC's seeming willingness to bury the hatchet (20) with the AIBD boded well for a satisfactory outcome. Some members of the AIBD had anyway become members of the London Stock Exchange, either in their own right or by participating in the ownership of its member firms in preparation for the Big Bang. A merger of Isro and the SEC was eventually agreed, subject to approval by the AIBD and Stock Exchange members, in September 1986, see Chapter 5.

It is the gilts market that the overseas securities houses seem to be primarily interested in. Because the market is to remain within the Stock Exchange, they have had to apply for membership. In 1984 the Stock Exchange set out detailed proposals for the overall structure of the gilt edged market after the Big Bang. The Bank of England (1985) then laid down its dealing and supervisory arrangements for the gilts market, in the light of comments on its draft proposals published in November 1984. As in the Stock Exchange, there are to be market makers and applications were invited by the Bank, by 3 May 1985, from firms wishing to become gilt edged market makers. This attracted a lively response from established international securities houses and from the British financial institutions and banks, who were forming investment banking subsidiaries and groups. No applications were, however, received from the major Japanese securities houses, largely because of the ongoing negotiations between the UK and Japanese monetary authorities, discussed in Chapter 1, over access to each other's domestic markets - the equivalent Tokyo markets being virtually closed for foreigners. Further applications are to be considered following the Big Bang. Prior to the Big Bang there had been eight brokers involved in the gilts market. The Bank approved 29 applications from firms wishing to become market makers and it is widely believed that there will be a major shake-out after the Big Bang, leaving between 6 and 15 market makers, because the market is not large enough to support such a number. Competition will, therefore, be intense and casualties are expected.

The Central Gilts Office has replaced its manual system of stock transfer with an electronic one and hopes to introduce an electronic payments system soon after the Big Bang. The Bank intends to supervise the capital adequacy of the gilt edged market makers and of the providers of ancillary services to the market makers - the Stock Exchange money brokers and the inter-dealer brokers (21). Capital adequacy will be judged in relation to risks of various kinds and, to facilitate supervision and ensure fair competition, gilt edged market makers are required to be established as companies with dedicated capital. Assurance will be sought, from parents and substantial shareholders, that they will accept ultimate responsibility for the liabilities of their market making entities. The Stock Exchange will be responsible for all other aspects of market supervision, including the capital adequacy of all other Stock Exchange members.

4.3 Shaking up the Retail Financial Services Sector

In 1984 the government demonstrated its commitment to promoting competition in the retail banking and financial services sector. The budget included several measures promoting a more even treatment of banks and building societies. Building society interest was paid net of a composite rate of tax, slightly lower than the basic rate, whilst banks paid gross interest on deposits. The banks had claimed that this conferred a competitive advantage on building societies, particularly in attracting tax paying investors. The budget did not remove the composite tax arrangement, as urged by the banks, but did extend it to bank deposits, though not to National Savings Bank deposits, with effect from April 1985. Another major difference between their tax treatment was in the rate of corporation tax. Banks were liable to the full rate of 52% whilst building societies paid a special rate of 40%, which had been imposed because of their mutual status. Their inability to pay dividends meant that they could not qualify for any corporation tax relief in this connection. Banks were, however, able to reduce their corporate tax liabilities further by claiming capital allowances on their leasing operations. The balance between these two factors was complex and contentious. The 1984 Budget also introduced measures to achieve a better balanced regime in this respect. It announced a phased reduction in first year capital allowances, which would reduce the tax advantages of leasing, and the progressive reduction, to 35%, of corporation tax, so that the special rate would cease to exist after 1985.

Additionally, in February 1984, the Inland Revenue announced, following a decision by Ministers, that profits which building societies realised on disposal of gilt edged and certain other stocks would, in future, be treated as trading income, rather than capital gains. This brought the treatment of societies into line with that of the banks.

Not only did 1984 witness the creation of a more level playing field with regard to the tax treatment of banks and building societies, but it also saw the publication of a White Paper on Trustee Savings Banks (22) and a Green Paper on Building Societies (23). Following consultations, the proposals in the White and Green papers became law in 1985 and 1986 respectively. They are designed to facilitate major changes in Trustee Savings Banks (TSBs) and building societies. Their proposals and some of their implications will be discussed, in turn, below.

The government announced its intent to introduce legislation to transform the TSBs into a public company in the 1984 Queen's Speech. Because the TSBs' ownership was anomalous, its flotation was not to be regarded as part of the privatisation programme and the proceeds from it would, therefore, remain with the group, facilitating its further expansion. The government did not believe that it owned the TSBs, although the Treasury, rather than the Bank of England, was directly responsible for them. Further, they were not mutual organisations and were consequently not regarded as being owned by their depositors.

The TSBs originated, in the early nineteenth century, as thrift institutions, and the movement grew rapidly and spread throughout the UK and the Channel Islands. Their establishment and operations have been governed by a series of TSB Acts; the most recent and most important being that of 1976, following the 1973 Page Report on National Savings, which recommended that the TSBs be developed into a third force, alongside banks and building societies, in UK banking. In the 1960s, they developed from savings institutions towards fully fledged banks, introducing cheque accounts in 1965 and launching the TSB Unit Trust in 1968. The Central TSB (CTSB) was incorporated in 1973, to act as banker to the TSBs and their associated organisations, and in 1975 it became a functional member of the London Bankers Clearing House. It was a wholly owned subsidiary of TSB (Holdings) Ltd and, as banker to the regional TSBs, it became a recognised bank under the 1979 Banking Act.

The first major change in the TSBs' scope of operation occurred in 1976, when government control over the TSBs was relaxed and the most restrictive statutory limitations on their activities were removed. They were, for example, permitted to lend to the public for the first time. After 1976, the number of individual banks was reduced and rationalisation by regional amalgamation took place. By December 1983 there were only four TSBs: TSB England and Wales, TSB Scotland, TSB Northern Ireland, and TSB Channel Islands (TSBCI). These regional TSBs, which make up the TSB group along with the CTSB and the subsidiary companies, have a combined network of over 1650 banks, ranking them alongside the larger banks and building societies. The group's assets were comparable with the latter as well. They had over 6 million customers and 13 million accounts, which was more than either NatWest or Barclays.

The TSB group continued to diversify its range of services in the 1970s and 1980s, introducing credit card services, through their Visa affiliated TSB Trustcard Ltd, in 1978 and purchasing the United Dominions Trust finance house in 1981. It also introduced insurance broking, mortgage lending, investment management and other retail financial services and kept abreast of developments in electronic banking by introducing a network of Speedbank ATMs. Its 1,100 cash dispensers are to link into the NatWest and Midland network by 1988. It has become one of the UK's top 10 unit trust managers and the third largest issuer of bank credit cards. In 1979 it was permitted to lend to corporate customers and has since concentrated on developing quality business. It plans, following flotation, to establish 300 specialist offices to provide services to corporate customers. It has also been actively developing correspondent relations with overseas banks.

The TSB group, therefore, had developed a diversified range of services, a strong customer base and a large branch network by 1984. Compared to the other banks it was underlent, poorly represented in the South, and had a small amount of business with the corporate sector, professionals, and the middle and upper social groups, its clientele being predominantly in the C1 and C2 groups. It had plenty of room to expand and flotation would double the capital at its disposal. As well as developing corporate business, it aimed to become a financial supermarket for the retail customer. It had already invested heavily in technology, being the only major

UK banking group with computer terminals at its counters that can instantly summon and update details of customers' accounts, and had been modernising its branches and moving them to prime high street sites. The additional capital could, however, be used for acquisitions, to enable it to fill gaps in its range of services and extend its branch network in the south of England. One possibility might eventually be a merger with a building society (24) and talks are known to have taken place.

The TSB Act, passed in 1985, laid down the procedure to enable TSB to be floated and provided for the TSB to be covered by the 1979 Banking Act, and, therefore, to be supervised by the Bank of England, following its transformation into a public company. Flotation was originally planned for February 1986 but was delayed because some of its depositors fought a lengthy legal battle claiming effectively that, despite the 1985 Act, the depositors owned the bank. On 3 July 1986, five Law Lords dismissed the claim by depositors that the TSBs' surplus assets belonged to them. 21 July 1986 was designated vesting day and on that date the bank was transferred to the private sector, as part of the preparations for stock market flotation laid down in the 1985 Act. The TSBs and their associated operating companies became subsidiaries of a holding company called TSB plc and a flotation date for the group, excluding TSBCI, was set in September 1986. TSBCI was to be floated, as a wholly owned subsidiary, on the Unlisted Securities Market in November 1986. In line with the government policy of encouraging wide share ownership, TSB plc was encouraged to attract over 1 million shareholders. It was the largest non-government share offering on the UK Stock Exchange and is expected to raise about £1.6bn. It was felt that expectations could potentially be disappointed by: the requirement to achieve wide share ownership, the bank's decision to deter foreign investment, and the choice of a September flotation date, which is towards the end of the summer vacation period. The date was chosen to allow flotation ahead of the Big Bang and the British Gas privatisation, scheduled for November. Initial reaction to the flotation was extremely encouraging, however. 1.4m customers and over a ½m other investors expressed an interest in applying for shares, immediately following the TSB's publication of the conditions of the share issue in August 1986 and before the publicity campaign had got into full swing. TSB officials began to fear that it could prove too successful and that they could end up with more than 3 million shareholders on the register, making it costly to manage.

The full text of the Law Lords' ruling was published later in July and caused the government some embarrassment. It stated that the assets of the four TSBs had, until the 1985 Act, belonged to the State, subject to depositors' contractual rights, contrary to opinion at the time. This raised a storm of protest from the Labour Party, which pointed out that the government had consequently sanctioned the sale of £10m worth of public assets to speculators, allowing the proceeds to accrue to the bank rather than the Exchequer. They called for a Parliamentary debate and postponement of the flotation. Meanwhile the depositors decided to consider the possibility of taking the case to the European Court of Human Rights. The government remained adamant that the flotation should go ahead, and Mr Ian Stewart, the Economic Secretary to the Treasury, drew attention to the legal distinction between the Crown, the government and the State.

The Labour Party's case was seemingly supported unwittingly by the Solicitor-General, Sir Patrick Mayhew, in a reply to Labour's legal affairs spokesman, John Morris, who had sought his opinion on the Treasury's view of the Law Lord's judgement delivered in a speech by Lord Templeton. Mayhew wrote that he agreed with the Treasury's distinction between the State and government in the case of TSB ownership and argued that, consequently, the proceeds of the sale need not go to the Exchequer, as would those from a privatised company. He added, however, that there was no legal personality entitled to the TSB's assets and Parliament was free to dispose of them as it thought fit. The shadow Chancellor, Roy Hattersley, argued that Parliament had not had the opportunity to debate the issue in the light of all the options available and, in particular, that it could have decided to donate the proceeds of the sale to the Treasury. Morris considered taking the matter to the Parliamentary Commissioner, who acts as ombudsman, to investigate Labour's allegations of faulty administration on the part of the government.

More careful consideration of the text of the Law Lords' ruling indicated that Lord Templeton's legal usage of the term State in fact implied that the ownership resided in an institution of the State. This had been clarified in a speech by Lord Keith of Kinkel, which explained what Parliament had intended by the 1976 and 1981 TSB Acts. The 1976 Act had set up an institution of the State, the TSB Central Board, which was legally distinct from the Crown or the government. When a TSB was closed its surplus was to be paid to the Central Board and under the 1981 Act this was to be distributed, at the discretion of the board, to the remaining TSBs. It was clear that there was no legal basis for any claim by a depositor against the board. The 1976 and 1981 Acts had not considered the possibility that the board itself would be liquidated, leaving this for future legislation. The 1985 Act decided to transfer the surplus assets of the statutory TSBs to the successor companies set up under the privatisation scheme. The Act, therefore, did not provide for the transfer of either the government's or the depositor's assets to the successor companies. Only the public, through its State institutions, had any claim on the assets and Parliament, on their behalf, decreed that they should be transferred to privatised companies. The Solicitor-General's opinion, and therefore the Treasury's, thus appears to be correct. Because Parliament has already debated the provisions of the TSB Acts, Labour's allegations appear to be groundless. MPs may not have fully appreciated the legal implications of the legislation passed but this is almost certainly not the first time that this has happened.

The danger for TSB plc was that the flotation's success could be impaired by the political controversy. With Parliament in recess, however, it seemed likely that the storm would blow over and flotation would proceed as planned with resounding success. In the event, this was the case. The share offering was heavily oversubscribed and allocations were rationed. TSB raised about £1.5bn and ended up with about 3m shareholders on its register - probably more than it had originally wished for but, due to rationing, considerably less than the 5m or so that had actually applied for shares.

Competition between the banks and building societies had been hotting up in the 1970s and early 1980s. The societies had competed amongst themselves by building up their branch networks, price competition being ruled out until the ending of their effective interest rate cartel in 1984, when Abbey National had broken ranks. Since then they have competed on both lending and borrowing rates and devised attractive new savings schemes and there has been a sharp deceleration in the rate of branch expansion. They proved extremely successful, largely at the expense of the banks, in the savings market and built up their share significantly in the 1970s and early 1980s. They also began to offer money transmission services towards the end of the 1970s and, in the early 1980s, introduced interest bearing cheque accounts, but they were not empowered to offer cheque guarantee or credit cards. In the early 1980s the major clearing banks launched a counter attack. They moved into the mortgage market and rapidly built their share up to 26% in 1982. After this they withdrew somewhat but generally adopted a policy of expanding their retail base following their preoccupation with international banking in the 1970s and their reaction to the 1982 Mexican debt crisis. They began to offer more attractive accounts, introduced 'free banking' (25) in 1985, and some of them decided to open some branches on Saturdays. They also realised that home loan provision offered the opportunity of cross selling other financial services and become more seriously and permanently involved in providing mortgages, trying to regain some of the ground they had lost since 1982. By 1985 they had, with the help of the 1984 tax changes, started to increase their share of savings deposits, relative to building societies.

To encourage greater competition between banks and building societies and to provide the latter with greater opportunities to cross sell financial services, in order to create a more level playing field, the government published a Green Paper (26), in July 1984, proposing a new framework for building societies. Following consultations, the government published its revised proposals in the Building Society Bill of December 1985. A version amended by Standing Committee A was published in February 1986 and the Building Society Act was passed in July 1986. It is to become law with effect from 1 January 1987.

As a result of this legislation the building societies will be allowed to diversify into estate agency, real estate investment and development, and unsecured personal lending. They will also be able to extend their insurance broking services, which have developed in connection with their links with life assurance companies concerning endowment mortgages, and their involvement in money transmission services. The latter will be facilitated by their ability, by virtue of being allowed to undertake unsecured lending, to issue cheque guarantee cards. Additionally, in connection with the government's proposals for pension provision in the Social Services Bill, the government announced in May 1986 that it was to allow the societies to administer personal pension contracts on behalf of employees opting out of company pension plans or the State Earnings Related Pension Scheme (SERPS). Particip-ation in the personal pensions market, which may involve managing equitites and gilts, will bring societies closer to the mainstream of changes in the City associated with the Big Bang. It may also disturb their previously harmonious relationships with insurance companies. They do already have skills in this area, given their experience in managing their, often large, gilts portfolios, but may decide, initially at least, to work in partnership with insurance companies, earning fee income, rather than to administer pension schemes directly. The Act anyway restricts the extent to which they are allowed to diversify, as detailed below, and other activities may be given a higher priority. The societies were also given permission to administer Personal Equity Plans (PEPs), following their introduction in the 1986 Budget. This too would involve them in the management of equity portfolios.

The societies vary considerably in size. Even following a series of mergers, especially among smaller societies, there were still over 150 societies in 1986. The top five, however, accounted for over 55% of the total assets of the movement. The extent to which they take advantage of their new opportunities is likely to vary with size. The small and medium sized societies are expected to shy away from the risks involved in unsecured lending and are unlikely to get involved in pension provision, either individually or in consortia. The banks find unsecured lending one of their more profitable activities and the larger societies are unlikely to resist the temptation of developing in this direction. Because of the experience they have gained through their association with life companies and managing their gilts portfolios, they may even diversify into pensions and PEPs. Insurance broking will be a natural development for most societies and so too will estate agency, given past associations with the latter profession.

The Green Paper had proposed that societies be allowed to diversify into conveyancing. This would have had the effect of breaking up the solicitors' monopoly, in line with general government policy of promoting competition, and reducing house purchase costs, in line with the government policy of encouraging wider home ownership. The Law Society, with the backing of Lord Hailsham the Lord Chancellor, persuaded the government to turn back.

They drew attention to the potential conflict of interest between the societies' dual responsibility to the house purchaser and vendor. The societies' representatives argued that 'Chinese Walls' (27) could be erected, which were to be permitted elsewhere in the financial services sector under the new investor protection legislation (28), and that there should be little problem if commissions were disclosed to clients. The societies' dream of offering a one stop house trading service was, therefore, shattered. They will, however, be able to offer conveyancing through subsidiaries in which they have a minority stake and to non-borrowers. They can, therefore, build up experience in this area pending further changes which are permitted, at the discretion of the Lord Chancellor, under the Act. Although Lord Hailsham has chosen to use his powers restrictively, this may not be the case when a new Lord Chancellor takes office.

The new legislation permits societies initially to diversify their activities to include: a maximum of 5% of Class 3 assets, such as unsecured loans, residential property investment, estate agency investments, insurance brokerage interests and other subsidiary activities; a maximum of 10% of Class 2 assets, such as secondary mortgages; and at least 90% of their assets must be first mortgages to owner occupiers. They are, therefore, to be confined primarily to their traditional business. The Building Society Commission (BSC), which is to take over the supervisory role of the Chief Registrar of Friendly Societies and to be given a much wider range of powers, was permitted to raise these ceilings, for individual societies, to 20% for Class 2 and 10% for Class 3 assets.

Another major development has been the increasing recourse by societies to wholesale funding. The 1985 budget had permitted them to pay interest gross to overseas investors from April 1986. Given the practice of paying interest gross in the Eurobond market, they had been unable to tap it. As a result of the change the major societies started to issue perpetual FRNs (29) in September 1985. Prior to the 1986 Act they had to discuss plans to raise more than 5% of their liabilities in the wholesale market with the Registrar. The Act set an initial maximum of 20% on funds from the wholesale markets and the BSC was empowered to raise the limit to 40%. 80% of societies are expected to reach the 20% limit within 5 years. The attraction of the wholesale market to the societies is that it offers them both cheaper funds and the opportunity to achieve better matching by borrowing longer term. Previously they had largely been restricted to borrowing short to lend for often very long terms. They have also tried to improve matching by developing high interest accounts, with penalties on access, and issuing term savings bonds.

The larger societies feel that, to compete effectively with banks, they must rapidly develop their unsecured lending business and MTS services as well as the more peripheral retail financial services. The 5% limit is, therefore, viewed by them as being extremely restrictive. Additionally, some anomalies still remain in their tax treatment vis-à-vis banks and other new competitors in the home loans market. In the last four months of 1986, in order to attract sufficient deposits to meet the demand they faced for home loans, they were, for example, paying depositors 2% above wholesale market rates and the bank base rate. Their position had admittedly been made worse by the large withdrawals they had suffered as a result of the TSB and British Gas flotations. Many depositors in the domestic wholesale markets, such as pension funds, are tax exempt and Eurobond holders pay no tax. Lenders and borrowers on the wholesale market effectively split the tax exemptions between them and this is reflected in the lower rates. The societies' access to the market is, however, restricted and they are consequently in danger of finding their mortgage rates undercut by lenders able to raise the majority of their funds on the wholesale markets. They cannot respond by pushing down their savings rates because of competition from National Savings products, which are exempt from the composite rate of tax, and banks, which have greater access to the wholesale markets. If such anomalies prove serious, however, government action is to be expected given its policy of encouraging wider home ownership. The home loan market remains protected. This was demonstrated by a Bank of England's 1986 ruling concerning Kleinwort Benson, the merchant bank. It proposed to offer mortgages in excess of requirements for house purchase and home improvements as a form of cheap secured lending to selected clients. The Bank ruled that it contravened its 1982 directive restricting banks to offering mortgages for house purchases and improvements.

The larger societies are likely to have greater access to the wholesale markets and this will add to their competitive edge. Many commentators have forecast a further increase in concentration, especially through mergers amongst the smaller societies, following the Act. There will be pressure to achieve economies of scale, given the introduction of new technology, and rationalisation is clearly possible, given the large and overlapping branch networks. It has been widely forecast that by the year 2000 there will be only five major societies operating alongside twenty smaller ones, which will act in partnership with other financial institutions. The larger societies may by then have converted themselves into public companies, in order to get round the restrictions embodied in the 1986 Act. If they do, they will be required to apply for banking licences under the 1979 Banking Act and will come under the supervisory wing of the Bank of England. It is a moot point whether they will wish to be called banks but they will effectively have become banks.

The 1984 Green Paper adopted a permissive stance towards their conversion from mutual societies to public companies. In the weeks prior to the Bill's publication in December 1985, conversion became a major topic of interest as Abbey National and other societies declared that they might want to escape the Bill's restrictions by going public. The Green Paper had proposed that societies should be able to allocate shares in the new company free of charge, if the members approved. This was later realised to be open to abuse because it would probably provide a large windfall for investors who could switch funds into societies preparing to go public. This had occurred in the US prior to the regulation introduced in 1976 concerning the conversion of savings and loan associations. The UK Treasury's response was to issue a consultative document on conversion, at the same time as the Bill, which it hoped would lead to its amendment. The document's proposals included restrictions which went well beyond removing the scope for abuse.

The underlying problem is that the owners of a society's reserves were regarded, by the Green Paper, to be its investors at the time of conversion. These reserves, however, represent a society's accumulated surplus throughout history, some of the contributors to which have died. The consultative document proposed that investors of two years standing prior to conversion and who remained investors for two years following conversion should be entitled to some of the benefits of ownership. The remaining surplus would belong to the society itself. Conversion would, therefore, endow the society with substantial capital. Such a proposal would of course give a further incentive for conversion. Perhaps to counter this the Treasury proposed that 20% of all those entitled to vote should approve conversion. The major societies have argued that this effectively bars conversion since they are lucky to get a response as high as 10%, even for votes concerning merger proposals which attract extensive publicity. Further, in the case of societies wishing to convert prior to acquisition by banks, such as the TSB, the Royal Bank of Scotland, Citicorp and Standard Chartered, which might wish to expand their branch networks, the virtually prohibitive requirement of 50% investor approval was proposed. Such proposals effectively impede the rationalisation of the financial services sector, which appears necessary in the light of the numerous overlapping branch networks, each offering increasingly similar arrays of services, that could result from the government's initiatives in the retail banking sector. Efficiency as well as competition should be encouraged. It really only seems necessary to prevent societies from being purchased at a discount. Rationalisation is also impeded by the fact that the Bill requires mergers between societies to be approved by 20% of each society's members.

Conversion would not only endow societies with capital, under the Treasury document's proposals, but allow them to tap new sources, such as the Stock Exchange, and to expand their wholesale funding. There is a suspicion that they are currently undercapitalised and the Registrar advised them, in 1985, to concentrate on bolstering their reserves. They have about half the capital underpinnings of banks. It is probably due to this inadequacy that the restrictions have been imposed on their new business opportunities. In the 1980s they have had to invest a great deal of capital in new equipment, to keep pace with technological developments in the banking sector (30). In August 1986 the Registrar issued a consultative paper on capital adequacy and announced that a paper on liquidity regulation would be published by the BSC, which was to take over as the supervisory body in September, before the end of the year. The capital adequacy paper warned societies against a further reduction in their liquidity, which had been run down toward the accepted minimum norm of 15% of total assets in 1986. It also proposed a system for assessing capital adequacy, which was consistent with that applied by the Bank to banks, to replace the eighteen year old system of prescribed reserve ratios. The proposed capital requirements were graded by class of asset, the least risky (class 1) assets requiring less backing than more risky ones. The Building Society Association (BSA) complained that the rules were too restrictive. It argued that they would discourage diversification into the new business permitted by the Act and were too tough generally, because of the low rating given to property as a capital asset and an excessive requirement to depreciate the value of their gilts holdings, to cover for possible capital losses when interest rates rise. The BSC was to consider the BSA's criticisms and publish a final set of rules by Christmas 1986. If the requirements are not eased the BSA will seek permission to issue more subordinated debt and ask the BSC to treat it as capital.

By virtue of the 1986 Act, building societies will be permitted to diversify into the various new activities from 1 January 1987. The Act, however, postponed the date from which building societies will be allowed to convert from mutually owned societies to public limited companies until 1 January 1988. The postponement was to allow further consultation and preparation before detailing regulations governing conversion. The restrictions imposed by the Act imply that, if their share of the increasingly competitive home loans market falls, they must restrict their other business accordingly. The development of a secondary home loans market and a secondary market in unsecured loans would allow them either to buy more mortgages or to sell unsecured loans, thus increasing their flexibility. The process of securitisation has opened up the prospect of such developments. In the next section: the potential development of a secondary mortgage market in the UK; some other important developments affecting the UK banking system; and the possible implications of deregulation for the UK banking system in the short term will be discussed.

4.4 Other Deregulatory Developments

In the 1980s, as we noted above, competition has increased in both the savings and home loan markets. Competition in the savings market was heightened not only by the clearing banks' decision to try to win back custom from the building societies, but also because of the government's decision to raise the contribution of National Savings to its funding. The government proved innovative in this field, introducing a series of more attractive savings instruments, including indexed linked savings certificates. The increase in competition in the home loans market has possibly been even more marked. Apart from the new interest in home loans shown by the clearing banks, there have been a number of other new entrants to the market. These have included: foreign and merchant banks, which have tended to concentrate on large mortgages provided as part of a package to high income clients; insurance companies, which have regarded home loans as a natural extension of the endowment policy business developed through their links with building societies; and specialist home loan finance institutes which rely on wholesale funding.

In the mid 1980s four specialist mortgage companies were established amidst a blaze of publicity. They committed themselves to transforming the way in which UK home loans are funded. Their initial impact was, however, not as great as expected. The National Home Loans Corporation (NHLC) was launched in September 1985 with a stock market listing and plans to raise £100m. Its initial strategy was to buy portfolios of existing mortgages from local authorities, which it believed would jump at the opportunity of realising such assets given the financial strictures they faced. In the first six months it ran into difficulties in meeting its targets for acquiring mortgage assets. Its main source of business has instead been individual borrowers referred to it by insurance companies keen to sell endowment policies tied to its mortgages.

Despite the removal of the Life Assurance Premium Relief in the 1984 Budget, which was supposed to eliminate a bias towards savings through life insurance, there was a boom in mortgage related life business in the mid 1980s. The top four life insurance companies involved saw their business double in the first six months of 1986, compared with a similar period in 1985. The 1984 tax reform had allowed tax payers to continue to benefit from the tax free lump sum, often exceeding the value of the house because of the inclusion of bonuses, payable at the end of the mortgage period. In 1986 the major building societies dropped their practice of charging an interest premium on endowment, as opposed to standard repayment, mortgages. Because only interest is paid during the life of an endowment mortgage, the fall in interest rates has also increased their attractiveness compared to standard repayment mortgages, which include both interest and capital repayments. With interest rates standardised, the lump sum benefit has become decisive and the building societies have been promoting endowment mortgages to earn fee income for insurance companies. Not surprisingly, the major insurance companies have been tempted to try to cut out the middle man by referring customers directly to the new home loans companies such as NHLC. The US banks moving into the UK mortgage market have also picked up business from life companies.

Another specialist entrant was the Mortgage Corporation, which is the subsidiary of Solomon Brothers, the New York investment house which is one of the leading players in the US mortgage backed securities market. So far it has picked up business from insurance companies but it intends to assign, to direct applicants, mortgage consultants, with whom they will deal over the telephone. Kleinwort Benson, the UK merchant bank, entered the market in 1984 and has introduced a series of innovative services. Its attempt to supply secured lending was, however, blocked by the Bank of England in 1986, as noted above. Since then it has set up a company called the Mortgage Funding Corporation. It does not intend to sell mortgages to borrowers directly. It is offering to supply funding to banks and other mortgage companies wishing to limit the mortgage assets they carry on their balance sheets. The funds will initially be raised through its banking facilities and later through FRNs, fixed rate Eurobonds using Swap facilities and possibly a Euro-commercial paper programme. Finally, so far, the Household Mortgage Corporation, which was given £25m of capital by several large financial institutions led by Mercantile House Holdings, plans to start offering mortgages from September 1986. Like NHLC it will use insurance companies and brokers to reach borrowers, at least initially.

Apart from these specialists, another new entrant to the market will be the National Girobank, the Post Office's banking subsidiary. The Post Office announced record profits for 1985-6 for both postal and Girobank business. It hopes to diversify Girobank's activities and to attract £100m worth of business, by offering mortgages across Post Office counters, in the year beginning Autumn 1986. Applicants will be informed immediately, about their prospects of getting a mortgage, by phoning the Girobank after having picked up initial information from a Post Office. It is expected that many of the Girobank's 2m current account holders will be interested in switching their mortgages. The Post Office is also to invest heavily in counter automation to improve both Post Office and Girobank services.

The specialist home loans companies are also potentially significant actors in the personal sector loan market. Under current regulatory arrangements they will not be supervised by the Treasury or the Bank of England. Consequently, unlike Kleinwort Benson, they will be able to offer revolving secured loan facilities which home owners could tap to fund their consumer spending. Their major impact may, however, be to develop a market in secondary mortgages or mortgage backed securities alongside the US banks, which have experience in the US secondary mortgage market. This will allow them to separate and, when desirable, to offload the three traditional functions of building societies: raising money; lending it to home owners; and servicing the loan. The market has not so far taken off because their operations were curtailed by the general cut in mortgage rates in 1986, which has led to much finer margins above the wholesale money market rates which they have to pay for their funds. The financial markets were still awaiting the first issue of mortgage backed securities in mid 1986.

Issues of mortgage-backed securities to institutional lenders such as insurance companies should allow the specialist institutions to raise cheap funds for lending. They are expected to concentrate on lending to the most creditworthy home owners, in order to minimise risks. The consequences, for the building societies, may be not only increased competition but increased risk, as they are left to deal with less creditworthy borrowers. The societies have hitherto paid higher rates to savers than they have for funds raised on the wholesale market and could force the specialist institutions out of the markets by cutting savings rates to levels below wholesale rates. In so doing they would, however, risk losing some of their savers to banks and would remain constrained by restrictions on their wholesale funding. It, therefore, seems likely that the specialist home loan companies will remain in business, even if the margin between savings and wholesale rates, which has so far inhibited their profitability, remains fine, because of the low costs involved in their operation. They do not have expensive branch networks to maintain and they do not have to undertake expensive advertising campaigns to compete with banks and building societies in the savings market. They have established themselves without branch networks by dealing with mortgage brokers, insurance companies and direct applicants. Other possible distribution media, such as estate agents, have not yet been tapped. They would dearly like a market in mortgage backed securities to develop to complement their wholesale funding.

The rapid growth in the early 1980s of the US secondary mortgage market, in which mortgages are repackaged into securities for resale to investors, has caught the imagination of the City as it has considered new avenues for the process of securitisation. In the US, the sale of new mortgage backed securities more than tripled between 1981 and 1984 and an active secondary market in the securities has developed. The secondary mortgage market had grown steadily under the wings of three government sponsored agencies: the Government National Mortgage Association (Ginnie Mae); the Federal National Home Loan Corporation (Freddie Mae); and the Federal National Mortgage Association (Fannie Mae), which either insure or guarantee mortgages. Its growth spurt in the early 1980s resulted from the credit crunch faced by the savings and loan asociations (SLAs) as deregulation pushed up short term funding costs. Because US home loans had traditionally been fixed interest rate ones, the costs of short term funds rose above revenues from long term loans. They turned to the federal agencies for help in restructuring their portfolios by repackaging unprofitable fixed rate mortgages. Since then the number and variety of mortgage backed securities has proliferated, as a result of innovations introduced by Salomon Brothers and First Boston, which dominate the US market, and the SLAs have pushed adjustable rate mortgages. The rapid emergence of a secondary mortgage market in the US has owed much to the intrinsic tradability of fixed rate mortgages. Variable rate mortgages are non-standardised and some Wall Street analysts believe it could be years before a large secondary market for such mortgages emerges. Developments in the UK, where variable rate mortgages are prevalent, will thus be watched with interest.

The impetus for developing a secondary mortgage market in the UK resulted from the Thatcher government's policy of encouraging local authorities to sell off their council houses. This resulted in the authorities making billions of pounds worth of mortgages which some wanted to sell to release capital for other pressing needs. The NHLC was established to take advantage of this opportunity but soon found that it had overestimated the amount of business forthcoming, at least in the short run, largely because the assets have been producing good profits for the local authorities. In the future the specialist organisations may be able to purchase home loans from banks and other institutions wishing to restructure their portfolios. The banks had, after all, expanded their share of the market once, then run it down, and then decided to expand it again in the space of four years in the early 1980s. The large banks may be more likely, however, to hive off mortgages to specially created subsidiaries in the future, especially if there is a downturn in the home loans market (31). Whilst the specialist institutions stand ready to purchase loans from the mortgage originators, who in many cases will continue to service the loans and set mortgage rates, the prospects for a fully fledged secondary market remain uncertain. The development of an active secondary market might, however, be encouraged by building societies. The restrictions on their asset portfolios, imposed by the Building Societies Act, mean that if their share of the mortgage market shrinks then the growth of their other, newly permitted, activities must be curtailed. They could, however, circumvent this restriction by buying more mortgages on the secondary market. The prudential implications of the increased competition in the home loans sector and the development of a secondary mortgage market will be discussed in the next chapter.

Another major development along the road to securitisation was the authorisation by the UK monetary authorities of a sterling commercial paper market in 1986. The implications of the development of commercial paper markets for the banking system were discussed in Chapter 1. Its authorisation required amendment of the 1979 Banking Act to exempt commercial paper from being defined as a deposit. This was a legal obstacle because deposit takers had to be licensed, under the Act, and companies wishing to issue the paper, and therefore take deposits, would have been required to apply to the Bank for a licence. The first paper was issued in May 1986 but by July it became apparent that the market had developed only slowly. Banks had been the major investors up to that date. Its initial development may have been inhibited by a number of factors. Many corporate treasurers may have held back until the Companies Act is amended to lift the requirement on issuers of securities to publish a prospectus. This was done in the Financial Services Act (32) and many feel that only subsequently will it be possible to gauge the true potential of the market.

There has also been concern that the price of the paper could be adversely affected by the Bank of England's attempts to reduce the commercial bill mountain, which grew as a result of the overfunding technique of monetary control abandoned in October 1985. Until the uncertainty caused by the size of the bill mountain is removed the market's development is likely to be inhibited. The commercial bill market, which grew appreciably in the first half of the 1980s as commercial companies effectively sold bank accepted bills to the Bank to raise finance, may well go into decline as the commercial paper market develops. Commercial paper is unsecured and its issuers are, therefore, assuming a higher risk than they incur through bank borrowing and the issuance of bills accepted by banks. It does, however, provide a cheap source of funds to creditworthy borrowers. The Bank has initially restricted the market to companies with assets in excess of £50m and has allowed issuers to set up bank credit lines in the event that they cannot repay or roll over the debts themselves. The minimum denomination of the paper has been set at £500,000. It is, therefore, to be a market for professionals. If these restrictions are relaxed there may be a role for credit rating agencies, such as Moody's and Standard and Poors in the US. The market's developments would be encouraged if a secondary market facilitating trade in the paper were to be established.

The secondary market in the US has remained small despite the explosive growth, in the 1980s, of the issue of commercial paper. The discount houses, which have actively traded in commercial bills, may, however, find the new business profitable as they explore new possibilities in the reformed capital markets, see below. The rapid growth in the Euro-commercial paper market, which made major inroads into business previously channelled through the Euronote markets in 1985 and 1986, indicates that the sterling commercial paper has good prospects. The paper market appears to be a natural home for corporate liquidity and if corporate treasurers come to this conclusion the body of investors should broaden beyond the banks. It is also likely to include the investment houses attracted to London by the Big Bang. Although the major clearing banks are set to lose working capital loan business as the market develops, they stand to gain fee income earned, through their merchant and investment banking subsidiaries, from placing the paper. With the major US securities houses gaining permission to deal in the market, however, competition will be intense. The US market is a low margin high volume business supporting about half a dozen large dealers. In the UK it is unlikey to grow to a size able to support all the current players and it too is likely to be dominated by five or six players.

The pace of change in the UK financial markets in the 1980s has, therefore, been rapid. New markets have been developing and the major banking institutions have been transforming themselves. Having diversified extensively and developed their international business in the 1970s the UK clearing banks had become more like German universal banks. They differed to the extent that they were not major shareholders in the corporate sector and did not deal extensively on the domestic securities markets. In the 1980s they have developed their investment banking subsidiaries: either internally, as in the case of Lloyds; or by acquisitions of jobbing and broking firms, which have been welded together with the appropriate divisions of their merchant banking subsidiaries to form US style investment banks. This has put them into a position to take advantage of the securitisation process that has emanated from the London based Euromarkets and begun to spread through the domestic financial markets and the opportunities provided by the Big Bang, particularly in the gilts markets.

The major merchant banks have also, usually via acquisition of brokers and jobbers, also developed investment banking divisions, to complement their more traditional merchant banking business, in order to meet the requirements of their corporate clients and to prepare themselves for the Big Bang. Some of the private merchant banks will maintain their status and look for niche business; others, such as Morgan Grenfell in July 1986, have gone public in order to raise the capital necessary to compete with the big banks and the US and Japanese securities houses.

The general picture is, therefore, one of major commercial banks developing into financial conglomerates, participating in investment and merchant banking business with the corporate sector and international banking business, on the one hand, and providing a whole array of retail financial services through financial supermarkets on the other. Their competitors in the corporate sector and the gilts markets will be the investment banking divisions of the merchant banks, foreign securities houses, and the investment banking divisions created in London by the major international banks. In the retail sector they will mainly compete with the smaller banks, the building societies, and possibly the more aggressive overseas banks. It is expected that the TSB and the building societies, after going public and perhaps merging amongst themselves or with banks keen to develop branch networks (33), will emerge as formidable adversaries in this sector. The major societies and the TSB are known to have plans to develop into retail financial supermarket chains. There will probably be room in the corporate sector for specialists seeking niche business and in the retail sector for financial boutiques, seeking to sell tailored services to the more discerning customers.

Discount houses, which are not found in any of the world's other major financial centres, have also had to adapt to the changes. They have enjoyed a protected status because the Bank of England chooses not to deal directly with banks. The discount houses alone have access to the Bank's discount window and the discount market acts as a buffer between the Bank and the banks. When the Bank wishes to supply reserves to the banks, or to withdraw reserves, it buys bills from, or sells them to, the discount houses which act as market makers in the Treasury and commercial bills markets. The Bank, therefore, undertakes its open market operations through the discount market and can relieve any shortages it creates in the market by supplying funds to the discount houses. It uses this relationship to influence interest rates. Whilst the Bank was attempting to control the money supply by overfunding, as described in Chapter 2, the role of the discount houses was called into question. Future changes in the operation of monetary control, involving the Bank dealing directly with the banks through the interbank markets, could further undermine their protected status. The revision in the structure of the gilts market, which took effect after the Big Bang, will allow UK and foreign banks to become primary dealers in the gilt edged market, which is the medium to long term market in government securities. This will allow them access to the Bank's gilts window as market makers in government debt. The banks also want access to the Bank's discount window, to enable them to trade in the market for government debt of less than one year and in bills. Banks are allowed similar access in the US and Germany for example. Only discount houses will be allowed access, as in the past, under the new arrangements but they will also be permitted to become gilt edged market makers. The banks are effectively barred from discount market business, although as primary dealers in the gilts market they will be able to bid for Treasury bills, and a question of fairness arises. The discount houses are further favoured by being allowed to run a larger book of securities for each £1 of capital than the gilt edged dealers. The continued separation of the short and the medium and long term markets is regarded by many as anachronistic.

Perhaps in response to allegations of favouritism, in July 1986 the Bank announced proposals for replacing 'club money'. The club money arrangement required UK banks to maintain a proportion of their assets in deposits with discount houses. This ensured that there was always sufficient liquidity in the banking system to keep it operating smoothly and that individual banks had ready access to money at call. In January 1984 the Governor of the Bank had announced that club money would have to go before the Big Bang in order to allow for the increased foreign banking presence. In its place, the Bank proposed new liquidity requirements on domestic and foreign banks in a paper published in July 1986 (34). The initial proposals suggested that the eleven major clearing banks might effectively take the place of the discount houses as the main holders of liquidity, with the other banks holding their liquidity in the form of deposits with a major clearer. The end of club money will deprive the discount houses of a plentiful supply of funds from banks. The houses themselves point out that the money was no longer all that cheap, relative to other sources, and that their profits should not suffer too much as a consequence.

As their name implies, discount houses have, in the past, been primarily in the business of buying short term promissory notes at a discount. They have funded themselves partly by taking money at call from the banks, partly by borrowing and partly by rediscounting eligible bills at the Bank. When the banking system has surplus short term funds it lends to the houses which then bid for bills and consequently drive down short term interest rates. Conversely, when the banks are short of liquidity lending dries up and the houses rediscount more bills with the Bank. If the Bank wishes to squeeze liquidity it can limit the volume of bills it accepts and, in the last resort, force the houses to borrow from it at a penal rate. The volume of business is large and their margins are thin. In the 1950s they dealt primarily in Treasury bills but since then bank and commercial bills have become the principal stock in trade. This was reinforced in the 1980s as the supply of Treasury bills was reduced to a trickle as the government funded itself increasingly in the gilts market, engaged in overfunding, and tried to raise larger amounts through National Savings instruments. By the end of 1984 Treasury bills accounted for just 3% of the market's sterling assets. Bank and commercial bills accounted for 44% and certificates of deposit for 28%. The development of the commercial bills market was actively encouraged by the Bank to provide an alternative to Treasury bills. In 1981 it significantly increased the number of banks eligible to accept bills that it would rediscount. By 1985 there were 128 such UK and foreign banks.

There was a contraction of the number of discount houses, from 13 in 1980 to 9 in 1985. In February 1985 Citicorp was allowed by the Bank to become the first UK or foreign bank to own a discount house. It bought Seccombe, Marshall and Champion, the second smallest member of the London Discount Market Association (LDMA) and broker to the Bank in the money market. Citicorp, however, had to agree to allow the house to operate as an independent subsidiary. Thus although the Bank was prepared to sanction further rationalisation in the market, and increased capitalisation from purchasing institutions, it was not prepared to see the houses absorbed into the treasury departments of banks. Following the Citicorp breakthrough, there have been further acquisitions of discount houses with the Bank imposing similar conditions. Soon after the Citicorp deal, Mercantile House, the large UK financial services group, bought both Alexanders and Jessel Toynbee which it merged. In March 1986 Clive Discount was taken over by Prudential Bache, a UK financial services group, and the smallest, Quin Cope, has been purchased by Banque Belge. There was also a merger of King and Shaxson with Smith St Aubyn in the mid 1980s. By mid 1986 only eight houses remained. Of these only four, including the three largest, remained independent. Outsiders have been interested in purchasing discount houses, in the build up to the Big Bang, because of both their experience as market makers and their sole access to the short term securities markets. The smaller houses desperately needed capital if they were to take advantage in the post Big Bang era of their opportunity to make markets in gilts and become primary dealers.

The market had become dominated by the three largest independents, which accounted for about 70% of the market's capacity. Thus, apart from the financial services revolution, there were pressures on the smaller houses to merge to keep up. The major discount houses already dealt, through jobbers, in short dated gilts, which at the end of 1984 accounted for 5% of their sterling assets. Four discount houses were among the 20 or so financial institutions that applied for recognition as primary dealers: Cater Allen (independent), Alexanders-Jessel, Union Discount (independent) and Gerrard National (in partnership with the stock broker James Capel, which is partly owned by the Hong Kong and Shanghai bank group). Gerrard National has subsequently decided to go it alone and bought Intercommodity, a commodity broker. The smaller houses have decided not to apply for primary dealerships but King and Shaxson has applied to become a gilt market money broker (35) instead. In July 1986, however, Union Discount, the second largest, decided to pull out of the gilts market. This reinforced the view that the houses were anachronistic and that they would eventually disappear as the short and medium term markets merged in the future. The Midland Bank appears to hold a different view, however, and, in 1986, announced plans to create the first new discount house in recent memory. The Chairman of the LDMA believes that rationalisation is now complete and that there may be more, rather than fewer, houses by 1988.

If discount houses survive the upheaval of the Big Bang and other changes in the money and capital markets it will be as high powered market makers. They are ideally placed to deal in a secondary market in commercial paper, should it develop, and should be able to build up their gilts business, at least at the short end. The commercial bills market may, however, go into decline as the Bank's demand has been considerably curtailed by the ending of overfunding and its desire to run down the bill mountain. The head of the Bank's money market division is anxious to give the discount houses time to adapt to the various changes and the closed shop they enjoy in the short term securities markets will be opened up at a pace that is evolutionary rather than revolutionary. Major changes in the discount market will, therefore, probably be postponed until a couple of years after the Big Bang and major changes in monetary control methods, involving more direct dealings with banks, will probably be considered after that. From 1988 it seems likely that the short term markets will be opened to the UK and foreign banks. The other major clearing banks have already discussed the possibility, with the Bank, of opening discount house subsidiaries and started to deal in the short term markets open to them, to gain experience. Until the Bank alters its monetary control methods, these subsidiaries will have to be sufficiently independent to satisfy the Bank's requirements.

The discount houses have been prearing for the upheaval since the change in monetary control methods announced in 1981. They realised that they would need to prepare for the withdrawal of the Bank of England's patronage and the removal of their privileged status. They accelerated their diversification, which started in the 1970s, into new lines of business and, after 1984, began to prepare for the Big Bang. Diversification has been into adjuncts to their existing busines, such as: leasing and futures (Union Discount); commodities and futures (Gerrard); and insurance and fund management (Cater). The acquired houses, such as Alexanders and Clive, are becoming components of investment banking groups whilst Seccombe and Quin Cope are seen as no more than entry tickets to the discount markets for their parent banks. Once the Bank ceases to require separate incorporation it seems likely that the houses that have joined larger groups will lose their identities. They have already been integrated into their parents as far as possible. The independents face a much more challenging future. If they are to remain independent they will have to withstand competition from much stronger rivals.

To conclude this chapter, possible scenarios for the post Big Bang future will be considered. Three possible outcomes have been suggested. There could be the equivalent of a nuclear explosion leading to financial panic and a crisis. This is most likely if it coincides with the onset of a bear market, as the reform of the New York Stock Exchange in 1975 did. This could lead to the replacement of the self regulatory system envisaged in the Financial Services Bill (36) with stricter regulation through an institution, akin to the Securities and Exchange Commission in the US, which would have formal legal backing. Such an outcome would be all the more likely if a Labour government had to pick up the pieces. The clearing banks would be the most likely survivors, following a flight to quality. Alternatively there could be a lift off, leading to a bolstering of London's position in the international markets and a proliferation of domestic personal share holding, especially if stamp duty were abolished. Gilt sales would become easier and a newly elected Labour, Alliance or coalition government might engage in a public investment programme. Finally it could turn out to be damp squib, resulting in an anticlimax and a reversion of the stock and gilts market to type. Even with reduced stamp duty and tax concessions, available through PEPs and the BES for example, widespread share ownership may not result. Small investors will have little clout in negotiating minimum commissions and may continue to be priced out of the market, as they are in the US where even discount brokers have minimum charges of around $45. Further an incoming Labour government might remove some of the tax incentives introduced by the Thatcher government. Other European capital markets might successfully compete for international business. Twenty-four hour global dealing in international securities may well evolve, but, whilst New York and Japan's position is largely unchallengeable by virtue of the size of the domestic economies and financial markets, London may have to share the European end of the business, with Frankfurt, Paris and Amsterdam in particular.

In the absence of a crisis, innovation is likely to continue in the wake of the Big Bang and greater use will probably be made of the newer financial markets in futures and traded options. These were established in the US in the mid 1970s and growth has been explosive in the 1980s. Financial futures and options provide opportunities to manage risks by facilitating hedging against risks caused by fluctuations in exchange and interest rates and stock prices. Futures contracts give the right and obligation to buy a security or currency at an agreed price on a preset date. Options give the right to buy but involve no obligation to do so. The impetus to the growth in financial futures and options markets has been exchange, interest rate and stock price instability. With inflation and interest rates falling and exchange rates possibly stabilising in the mid 1980s the initial propelling forces may dissipate, at least temporarily. The rapid growth in the markets, however, indicates that there will be sufficient demand to sustain future expansion, especially in London following the Big Bang.

The London International Financial Futures Exchange (Liffe) was established in September 1982.

In three years it had grown larger than the commodity futures exchanges, which had also been setting volume records, and had established itself as the largest futures market outside the US, although it was much smaller than the major US exchanges. Liffe offers contracts in gilts, equities, currencies and other securities. Its Financial Times-Stock Exchange (FT-SE) 100 contract has so far proved a flop but may take off after the Big Bang. In May 1985 Liffe and the Stock Exchange launched rival currency option markets. Liffe initially attracted a higher volume of trade but the Stock Exchange hoped to forge a link with the Philidelphia Stock Exchange, which leads in currency options, to establish itself as London's central market. Liffe is, however, developing its own links with other exchanges concerning currency and other futures and options. The Stock Exchange also offers options in gilts and equities. It introduced its traded options market in 1978 and, following a slow start, it experienced rapid growth in the mid 1980s and is expected to take off after the Big Bang. It aims to develop traded options on all major shares and expects a rapid growth in its gilt options business. The only concern about these developments is that they may lead to an increase in share price volatility. A study by the authorities responsible for supervising futures markets in the US has, however, concluded that they may actually stabilise prices. Further, they have the advantages: of increasing liquidity in the financial markets; and of shifting risks from those unwilling to bear them to those willing to assume them. Liffe has continued in its search for new contracts and is hoping to capitalise on London's central position in the Euromarkets. In 1986 it was trying to establish a Eurobond futures market, to allow issuers to hedge their positions following the losses incurred by Eurobond houses in the turbulent markets of the mid 1980s.

Whatever the outcome, London's importance as a financial centre seems assured as long as it can play host to the Eurodollar and other Euromarkets. The monetary authorities seem well aware of this and have been keen to ensure that the new self regulatory system does not push the business abroad. The new regulatory structure for the financial system will be discussed further in the next chapter. As far as the domestic, and especially the retail, financial services sector is concerned, it should be stressed that increased competition from building societies and the TSB and the influence of new technology are likely to prove to be at least as important as the Big Bang.

Notes

1. See Pecchioli (1983).
2. Banking ventures established by foreign banks in overseas banking centres.
3. An influential New York based independent research organisation.
4. See Chapter 1.
5. See Kraft (1984).
6. See Chapter 1.
7. See Bank of England (1985b) for an analysis of trade in services. It shows: the UK share of financial and non-financial services trade to have been declining; financial services to be a relatively small proportion of total invisible exports; and that the City's contribution to the net surplus in invisibles is a major one.
8. See The Observer, 6 July 1986, p.31.
9. See Terry (1985) for details.
10. See Terry (1985) for details.
11. This advantage of single capacity is judged by some to be overestimated, see Terry (1985) for further discussion.
12. See The Observer, 6 July 1986, p.36, for a history of mergers and acquisitions.
13. Draft rules were published in May 1986.
14. See Bank of England (1985).
15. Discussed in Chapter 5.
16. Which is to have powers delegated to it, by the Department of Trade and Industry, and will oversee UK investor protection, see Chapter 5.
17. The National Association of Securities Dealers and Investment Managers.
18. The International Primary Markets Association.
19. International Securities Regulatory Organisation.
20. It has been highly critical of Eurobond market trading practices.
21. Stock Exchange money brokers and inter-dealer brokers add to the liquidity of the markets. The former take surplus funds from sellers of stocks and lend them to buyers of stocks or place them elsewhere. Subject to the prudential guidelines, they will be permitted to deal in money market instruments and engage in inter-dealer broking, to provide dealing facilities between market makers.
22. Command Paper 9415 (1984).
23. Command Paper 9316 (1984).
24. See below.
25. The practice of not charging customers maintaining non-negative current account balances for money transmission services used. The major clearers had previously waived charges only if balances in excess of a non-negative minimum, e.g. £200, were maintained.
26. Command Paper 9316 (1984).
27. Figurative walls preventing departments, providing

particular groups of financial services, from exchanging confidential information with other departments, whose activities could benefit from the knowledge to the possible detriment of clients.

28. See Chapter 5.

29. Floating Rate Notes are Euronotes whose interest rates vary with market rates.

30. See Chapter 2.

31. See below.

32. Which was passed in July 1986, see Chapter 5.

33. Such as: Standard Chartered, which is a UK incorporated international bank seeking to create a UK network; TSB, which is under-represented in the South; and the Royal Bank of Scotland, which is anxious to develop a network in England and Wales.

34. See Chapter 5 for further discussion of liquidity requirements.

35. See note 21.

36. House of Commons (1985) 238.

Chapter Five

SUPERVISORY RESPONSES AND REGULATORY REFORM

5.1 Introduction

The 1979 Banking Act was a response to the 1977 European Communities (EC) banking directive (1) and the secondary banking crisis which occurred in the mid 1970s (2). The latter had demonstrated the inadequacy of the arrangement under which the major banks were informally supervised by the Bank of England and the secondary banks were overseen by the Department of Trade and Industry under Section 123 of the Companies Act. The 1979 Act made the Bank responsible for supervising the major banks, which became known as recognised banks, and the secondary banks, which became known as licensed deposit taking institutions (LDTs). In order to fulfil its wider supervisory role the Bank increased the size of its supervision division.

The 1979 Act gave statutory force to the Bank's supervisory responsibilities and for the first time legislated on bank authorisation and licensing, responsiblity for which would lie with the Bank. It permitted the Bank to continue with its traditional informal approach to the supervision of recognised banks whilst applying its new formal powers to the LDTs. The Act's main purpose was to protect depositors from loss and in this connection it required the establishment of a deposit protection scheme (3). The authorisation procedure was consistent with the EC directive and so too were subsequent guidelines, issued by the Bank, concerning liquidity and capital adequacy and foreign currency exposure (4).

The Bank has continued to respond to proposals of the EC Banking Advisory Committee (5) (BAC) and EC banking directives. Many of the members of the BAC are also members of the Committee on Bank Regulations and Supervisory Procedures, which meets at the Bank for International Settlements (6) in Basle and is also called the Basle Committee or the Cooke Committee (7). The Bank is represented on both committees which naturally make consistent pronouncements on supervisory and regulatory practices. In 1975 the Cooke Committee reached an agreement on the allocation of supervisory responsibilities between the regulators and supervisors in the countries in which foreign banks were operating and their countries of origin. This became known as the Basle Concordat. It was revised in 1983 (8), in response to further experience with the internationalising banking system. The revised concordat provided for supervision on a consolidated accounting basis (9) and a subsequent EC directive (10) has also required supervision on a consolidated basis. The Bank has stated (11) that it proposes to supervise on the basis of consolidated accounts wherever appropriate. The liquidity guidelines issued in the early 1980s (12) have had to be revised in the light of changes in the City in the run up to the Big Bang, as mentioned in the previous chapter. These changes will be discussed further in Section 5.2. The Cooke Committee has also investigated the implications of securitisation for bank supervision (13). It was especially concerned about the build up of off balance sheet risks and the lack of information about exposures. The Bank was quick to respond to its findings, publishing proposals in 1986, which will be discussed further below, concerning capital backing for off balance sheet risks. A related report (14), from a study group established by the central banks of the Group of Ten (15) countries, examined the implication of financial innovation for monetary policy. The UK monetary authorities are likely to have to adjust their monetary policy in the light of the report which implies that, with increasingly freer money and capital flows and the development of new liquid financial instruments, control of traditional domestic monetary aggregates is inappropriate. This may account to some extent for the shift in monetary policy towards exchange rate, rather than monetary aggregate, targeting.

The accelerated pace of change in the 1980s has not only led to a blurring of the distinctions between banks and non-bank financial intermediaries. It has also led to a reduction in the differences between recognised banks and LDTs. It was argued, by the Finance Houses Association (FHA) for example, that the distinction between LDTs and recognised banks detracted from the creditworthiness of the former, which were in fact more creditworthy than many recognised banks, and exposed them to discriminatory regulation. The FHA proposed that simple legislation should be introduced to cover deposit taking activities and that more comprehensive legislation should cover financial activities in general. The latter should build on the 1985 White Paper (16) on financial services and investor protection and the combined legislation should replace the 1979 Banking Act. Subsequent developments in banking and financial services legislation will be discussed in the next two sections. In the event, however, the Johnson Matthey Affair (17) demonstrated that the distinction between recognised banks and LDTs was outmoded, that a revision of the 1979 Act was required, and that the Bank's supervisory division needed to be further strengthened. These developments will be discussed in more detail in Section 5.2.

In the 1980s, the incidence of fraud in the City seemed to be growing. Public awareness of it was clearly heightened by the Johnson Matthey Affair and a series of cases involving the Lloyd's insurance market. New legislation (18) concerning Lloyd's was introduced, in 1982, in order to strengthen the regulation and supervision of the market but its troubles continued. There were calls for Lloyd's to be brought within the new financial services legislation which was being formulated but this was resisted by the government, which argued that time should be given to allow the provisions of the 1982 Act to take effect. In response to pressure from the opposition parties, however, it did agree, in January 1986, to set up an independent enquiry into the regulation of Lloyd's, despite the fact that an internal inquiry into the regulation and management of Lloyd's, led by Sir Kenneth Berrill, a member of the governing council and Chairman of the SIB, was in process. In reponse to City fraud in general a Fraud Investigation Group (FIG) (19) has been established and the Roskill Committee (20) has examined possibilities for adjusting legal procedures to make the prosecution of fraud easier.

The reform of the TSBs, discussed in the previous chapter, will have little impact on the supervisory structure. After privatisation they came under the Bank's wing, rather than the Treasury's. The building societies will, however, be more formally regulated and if any of them eventually go public they too will probably be overseen by the

Bank. These matters will be discussed further in Section 5.4.

The government's general approach to financial supervision has been one of introducing a new statutory framework that maintains the traditional flexibility of the UK supervisory approach. Hence the continued emphasis on self regulation, which should perhaps be called self supervision, within the evolving regulatory framework. This is consistent with the approach of the previous Labour government which introduced the 1979 Banking Act. There are those, including the current Labour opposition, who question the appropriateness of continuing with this approach in the increasingly complex and internationally oriented system that is developing. They feel that a more formal regulatory system is required with a statutory body, akin to the US Securities and Exchange Commission, at its centre. The return of a Labour government may, therefore, lead to further regulatory changes and even if the current Conservative administration retains power further changes may be required in the light of post Big Bang experience. These matters will be discussed further in Section 5.5.

5.2 Bank Supervisory and Regulatory Reform

The Latin American (LA) debt crisis (21) prompted central banks around the world, including the Bank, to urge domestic banks with exposure to country risks to increase their bad debt provisions and raise their capital ratios. The latter had fallen, by the early 1980s, to historically low levels, due to the rapid expansion of their loan business (22) and increased reliance on liability management. As the international banks withdrew from the international syndicated loan market, following the 1982 LA debt crisis, they not only looked to the development of their domestic business but also considered possibilities for asset management. New instruments were devised that effectively allowed them to trade loans and expand and contract their asset portfolios as required. This process of securitisation introduced new off balance sheet risks and bank supervisors had to respond to these new developments by reappraising their capital adequacy requirements. The Cooke Committee undertook a study of these developments and reported (23) in March 1986. The report identified and assessed the importance of the major sources of risk but stopped short of prescribing precise capital requirements, leaving this to the discretion of the supervisory authorities. In the same month the Bank published a paper outlining criteria from which it expected to develop, following consultations, formal new proposals on capital adequacy. It had, in May 1985, imposed an interim capital requirement on Nifs of half that applied to loans.

In 1985 the banks turned to the FRN market as a source of funding. The Bank had warned in 1984 that notes and other debt issued by other UK banks could not be included in a UK bank's capital base. The aim was to guard against increased bank interdependence. In December 1985 the Bank introduced new proposals concerning capital adequacy which covered conditions under which bank debt issues could be counted as primary capital. It argued that perpetual FRNs should only be counted if they carried the provision that they could be converted into ordinary shares should a bank run into difficulties. The banks felt this to be unnecessarily restrictive and that perpetual FRNs subject to these conditions would be virtually unsaleable. Their frustration was understandable because they thought that they had found an easy and cheap route to raise capital in response to the Bank's promptings. The Bank and the banks subsequently reached a compromise in 1985. Lloyds Bank issued a perpetual FRN which was convertible into preference, rather than ordinary, shares and which the Bank recognised as primary capital. The other major banks subsequently boosted their capital by issuing similar convertible FRNs.

Apart from developments in international banking and financial innovation, the 1984 Johnson Matthey Affair (24) has had a major impact on UK banking supervision. It highlighted the inadequacies of the practice of relying on independent auditors' reports without providing for an exchange of information between auditors and supervisors. In June 1984 the auditors had presented an unqualified report on the Johnson Matthey Bank (JMB) and yet on 1 October 1984 the Bank had to put together a rescue package for the bank. The affair also drew attention to the problem of supervising banks which are part of larger, not necessarily financial, groups of companies. The trend towards the formation of financial services groups and financial services divisions of other, especially retail, groups is likely to make the problem of regulating banks which are parts of conglomerates more common. In such cases it is insufficient to examine a bank's financial strength in isolation. The Bank has consequently stated (25) that consolidated supervision, hitherto applied to banks and their subsidiaries, should be extended to cover new relationships formed by banks and complement unconsolidated supervision.

Following the Johnson Matthey Affair (26), the Chancellor instigated an investigation of the bank supervisory system by a Treasury and Bank Review Committee. Its report (27) prompted the Chancellor to propose changes in bank supervisory arrangements in July 1985. A single authorisation procedure would replace the two tier system, which drew a distinction between LDTs and recognised banks, and the 1979 Banking Act would be changed accordingly. A regular dialogue would be permitted between the Bank and bank auditors. This would also require amendment of the Act and the agreement of the accountancy profession. Further, the Bank would be given additional powers to obtain information. In August 1985 the Bank issued a consultative paper developing the recommendations of the Treasury and Bank Review Committee, especially those concerning consultations between auditors and the Bank.

The Chancellor also proposed that loans to a single borrower should not exceed 25% of a bank's capital, except in exceptional circumstances, and that exposures exceeding 10% of capital would require greater capital resources than otherwise required. Banks were encouraged to strengthen their internal control and seek 'letters of comfort', pledging support from shareholders owning more than 15% of a bank. Additionally it was announced that the Bank's supervisory staff would be increased and more thoroughly trained.

A White Paper (28) followed in December 1985. It announced the government's intention to introduce a Banking Bill to revise the 1979 Act in the light of the Johnson Matthey Affair and the rapid changes occurring in the financial markets. Its main recommendation was the formation of a Board of Bank Supervisors to aid the Bank's Governor. The annual report to the Chancellor, made by the Bank under Section 4 of the Banking Act and laid before Parliament, will include a separate section by the Board giving an account of their work and expressing their view of current issues in the field of banking supervision. Its other recommendations were in line with those previously announced by the Chancellor and statutory backing for the guidelines on exposure was proposed. Exposures in excess of 25% of capital would require prior notification to the Bank. The White Paper's proposals aimed to preserve, as far as possible, the flexibility of the UK banking supervisory system and to complement proposed investor protection and building society legislation, to be discussed below.

Prior to the White Paper, in September 1985, the Bank had established a Bank Supervisory Committee consisting of the Deputy Governor, who is to be the Chairman, and four senior directors with specific responsibilities. One is to be responsible for banking supervision, one for Basle Committee co-ordination, another for home finance, and the fourth for securities and general finance. Additionally it was decided that the staff of the Banking Supervisory Division would be increased to 120 and receive additional training. In May 1986 the Chancellor approved five nominations by the Bank for membership of the Board of Banking Supervision. The Board is to advise the Governor and report separately to the Chancellor, annually. The Governor is free to ignore its advice but must report to the Treasury if he does so.

The proposals, in the White Paper on banking supervision and in the Financial Services Bill (29), to impose a statutory duty on auditors to act as watchdogs for fraud and to detect inadequate management control systems have caused unease both amongst management and within the accountancy profession. In June 1986 the Department of Trade and Industry (DTI) gave the latter twelve months to define the circumstances, such as suspicion of fraud, under which it was willing to bypass clients and report directly to supervisory bodies. The DTI reserved the right to lay down its own rules if those proposed by the profession proved inadequate.

The run up to the Big Bang also required the Bank to reconsider its arrangements for assuring the liquidity of the banking system. As mentioned in the previous chapter, it will no longer require banks to place 'club money' with the discount houses following the reform of the gilt-edged market. In a discussion paper issued in July 1986, it proposed instead to introduce a primary liquid asset requirement under which banks will have to hold a certain proportion of high quality liquid sterling assets, including cash and bills which the Bank will stand ready to buy. A two tier system is proposed. The eleven main clearing banks, the primary liquidity banks, will be obliged to hold their own liquid assets and secondary banks will be allowed either to hold their own liquid assets or to hold liquid assets in the form of deposits with the primary liquidity banks. The same liquidity formula will be applied to all banks, regardless of their size, because the cost of maintaining a liquid banking system should be fairly shared and individual banks will continue to be required to discuss their liquidity management with the Bank.

Also in connection with the Big Bang, the Bank issued a paper on supervision of securities business run by banks. It proposed rules on the organisation of banks' securities groups, to ensure that they are separately capitalised, in order to prevent securities trading losses from harming the parent bank, and to prevent conflicts of interest. Additionally, on 25 July 1986, the Bank issued a paper summarising its proposals to limit large loans by banks to individual borrowers. It is intended to complement the Banking Bill's requirement that banks should notify the Bank about large loans.

5.3 Investor Protection

The 1979 Banking Act was primarily concerned with depositor protection but, as noted in the previous chapter, the banks' share of the savings market declined considerably in the 1970s as savers placed an increasing proportion of their funds with building societies and with other financial institutions such as insurance companies and unit trusts. Directly or indirectly a larger proportion of savings were being invested rather than deposited and consideration, therefore, needed to be given to the protection of investors. In July 1981, the DTI asked Professor Jim Gower, its research advisor on Company Law, to review investor protection, following a series of scandals and the failure of several investment companies. The Gower Report (30), published in January 1984, recommended that there should be a body with some statutory powers, but answerable to the DTI, to oversee a limited number of self regulatory, professionaly based, organisations. The report saw the Council for the Securities Industry (CSI) as an existing body with potential for development into a statutorily backed umbrella agency overseeing self-regulatory agencies which might also have some statutory backing. The CSI was set up in March 1978 by the Bank as an umbrella body to supervise sectional interests within the City. It was much criticised by professionals, who claimed that it had little or no role to play. It had no statutory backing and in the 1980s the Bank took a more active role in surveillance, reducing the role of the CSI to that of an advisory agency.

Following the Gower Report, the DTI invited comments and in the light of these formulated proposals in a White Paper (31) published in January 1985, on which further comments were invited. The White Paper proposals were broadly consistent with the Gower Report proposals, except that two supervisory bodies were to be set up, raher than one, to oversee a number of self regulatory organisations (SROs). There appeared to be no role for the CSI. The two bodies were to be the Securities and Investments Board (SIB) and the Marketing of Investments Board (MIB).

The arrangements prevailing prior to the Gower Report revolved around the CSI and the Takeover Panel, an independent non-statutory organisation which produces and oversees a code of conduct concerning takeovers and related practices. The White Paper offered to give the Panel statutory backing if it felt it would be helpful in the future, in order to deal with a deregulated environment involving twenty four hour global markets and giant international securities groups. In 1985, the Panel published a paper considering a number of options ranging from independence to some form of absorption into the SIB. Its non-statutory form affords the Panel flexibility to respond to the changing environment, which it used in April 1985 to revise its code of conduct, and prevents it from having to defend its rulings in courts. The risks of inflexibility are demonstrated in the US where the merger wave of the 1980s has thrown up evidence of a number of unsavoury practices but the US Securities and Exchange Commission (SEC) and other regulators have been inhibited in their response due to legal obstacles. The Panel opted for independence but this may become untenable in the future. So far the US investment banks have followed its code scrupulously. Whilst maintaining its non-statutory and independent status, the Panel could be related more closely to the SIB, and/or the SROs, by having representatives from those bodies on the Panel. Additionally, authorisation by the SROs could be made conditional on promises to obey the Panel's code.

The White Paper did not finalise the regulatory structure. It left open the questions concerning the degree of reliance on self and statutory regulation and whether there would be one or two regulatory bodies. In addition no final decision was made on the degree of accountability of the bodies to the DTI or the split of responsibility for supervision between the DTI and the Bank. The Trade Secretary, it proposed, should however appoint an independent tribunal to act as final arbiter on any dispute about authorisation decisions and special provisions would be made, in the proposed legislation, to encourage competition in the financial services sector. The question of accountability of the bodies and their relation to the Secretary of State is an important one because the MIB in particular would have been responsible for a wide area of consumer protection. Further, the experience of the CSI showed that sufficient statutory backing for these bodies would be required to ensure that the City holds them in sufficiently high regard to prevent the need for the Bank to have to expand its supervisory authority into this area again. The worry is that without sufficient statutory backing there will not be enough checks and balances against established City interests.

The problem is one of striking a credible balance between self-regulation and statutory control. Under self-regulation, practitioners are supervised by regulators drawn from their own ranks. It has the advantage that specialists are more likely to detect bad practices but there is the disadvantage that professional self-interest might prevail over public, and especially investors', interests. A system based on self-regulation also requires a substantial input by the financial services industry itself and its response to this will largely determine whether the approach will work.

The Bank's primary interest in helping to formulate the new investor protection system seems to have been its likely contribution in securing the reputation of the City so that it can continue to evolve as a major international financial centre. The Bank in fact took a leading role in formulating the White Paper proposals. Following the Gower Report the Governor appointed an advisory committee to appraise responses to the Report.

The White Paper proposed that formal authorisation should be legally essential for advisors and companies involved in investment business. Powers of authorisation would be delegated by the Secretary of State of the DTI to the SIB and the MIB. The latter would be primarily concerned with packaged investments such as those provided through life assurance companies and unit trusts. The government would consider merging the two boards if the response invited to the paper indicated that the financial services industry and its customers would prefer such an arrangement. The boards would be able to recognise self-regulatory organisations (SROs), such as the Stock Exchange Council. The proposals were intended to assist in the enforcement of regulation, deter fraud and malpractice, improve disclosure, and lay down the principles of good business conduct. They were designed to build on the best of self regulation whilst providing some statutory backing to the supervisory system.

It proposed that the Chairman of the SIB should be appointed by the Secretary of State, with the agreement of the Governor of the Bank and that the Governor should appoint the remaining board members with the agreement of the Secretary of State. This power of veto, on the appointment of the Chairman of the SIB, by the Governor was severely criticised in the House of Commons debate on the White Paper, which generally favoured the proposals, as did the City. It also proposed that the Chairman of Miboc (MIB Organising Committee) should be appointed by the Secretary of State, along with the other members of the committee, in consultation with the financial services industry.

Initial reactions suggested that many businesses might have to register with both boards and proposed SROs, such as Nasdim (32), might also have to deal with both boards. The financial services industry was urged to formulate proposals for the new SROs by the end of the Summer of 1985, to meet the deadline introduced in the White Paper which envisaged that succeeding legislation would invest the SROs with powers to authorise financial companies in the Autumn of 1986, ahead of the Big Bang scheduled for 27 October 1986. It was pointed out that a new SRO would need a year from the autumn of 1985 to design and install its regulatory system to the standards required for recognition by the SIB or Miboc and that preliminary discussions with these bodies would be necessary.

A July 1985 briefing, by the Chairman of the SIB, identified clear gaps in the coverage of the SROs hitherto proposed, such as the Stock Exchange Council, Nasdim, and the Association of Futures Brokers and Dealers. Besides fund management, the SIB was thought to be concerned about the need for SROs to regulate foreign securities dealers, Eurobond traders and over the counter (OTC) market makers (33). It was also studying the corporate finance sector and a working party was set up, under the chairmanship of a leading merchant banker, to study plans for an investment management SRO. Miboc faced an even greater need to encourage the formation of

SROs. Nasdim also provides coverage in this area and the IBRC (34) existed as a statutory body but legislation was required to convert it into an SRO. Miboc faced the unique problem of dealing with thousands of assorted agents, brokers and salesmen, whilst the SIB would deal with more coherent groups in relatively small numbers. There was some criticism of the pooled investments grouping to be overseen by the Miboc. The unit trusts felt that they would be swamped by the interests of the insurance companies and the building societies were not represented. Subsequent to the White Paper a building society representative was appointed to the Miboc.

Following consultations concerning the White Paper, the Financial Services Bill was published in December 1985 (35). At the same time the SIB and Miboc published more detailed proposals about the operation of the regulatory structure (36) and the government published a consultative document on the role of auditors in the financial services sector.

The resulting legislation will make it a criminal offence for anyone to carry out investment business without authorisation. The Secretary of State for Trade and Industry is to be given powers to authorise and regulate the conduct of investment business and to be allowed to transfer the majority of these powers to one or more designated agencies. The agency or board would then be able to authorise parties wishing to carry out investment business and to recognise practitioner based SROs. Most investments businesses will be expected to join one or more of the SROs. To qualify for recognition the SROs will have to satisfy the agency that its rules, and their enforcement, will afford investors with protection at least equivalent to that provided by the agency. Professional bodies representing accountants and solicitors, which also carry on some investment business, will also be able to apply for recognition. An independent tribunal will be established to consider cases involving the agency's actions and the SROs will be required, as a condition of recognition, to establish their own independent appeals procedures. The Secretary of State will be given investigatory powers, including the ability to appoint inspectors to investigate suspected cases of insider dealing.

The document published by the SIB and Miboc envisaged one main board, with a wide range of powers delegated to it by the Secretary of State, having concluded that substantial advantages would flow from sharing their work load. The single board, yet to be named, would seek the transfer of all the regulatory powers in the Financial Services Bill capable of being exercised by a designated agency. It would focus on the protection of investors and the proper regulation of intermediaries. It would aim to keep the number of recognised SROs as small as possible in order to eliminate overlap and duplication and reduce problems of control and monitoring. It would also encourage businesses to obtain authorisation from SROs, rather than directly from the Board, and would set authorisation fees accordingly.

At the time there were seven SROs intending to seek recognition: the Stock Exchange; the International Securities Regulatory Organisation (Isro); the Association of Futures Brokers and Dealers; Nasdim; the Investment Management Regulatory Organisation (Imro); the Life Assurance and Unit Trust Regulatory Organisation (Lautro); and the Life and Unit Trust Intermediaries Regulatory Organisation. The SIB and Miboc had also discussed recognition with other organisations but felt that there was scope for merging some of the organisations to reduce their number. It was made clear that membership of an SRO would not give authorisation to conduct all types of business and that separate authorisation from the relevant SRO, or the Board, would be required for each type of business. In order to reduce the resulting complexity and to ensure adherence to liquidity, capital, and other rules it proposed to introduce lead regulators. These would be responsible for monitoring businesses which conducted the majority of their activities within their sphere of regulatory responsibility. It was, however, pointed out that close co-operation between SROs would be an essential part of the regulatory system and that SROs would have to commit themselves to share information in order to gain recognition. The lead regulator concept was also being discussed, by the SIB and Miboc, with other regulators, such as the Bank, and the DTI, which will remain responsible for supervising insurance companies under the 1982 Insurance Companies Act. They desired to minimise the duplication in reporting requirements on banks authorised by the Bank but also requiring authorisation from SROs or the Board in respect of their investment business.

The SIB/Miboc document also proposed a system of recognised investment exchanges (RIEs). An investment exchange is defined as a body which provides an organised market framework within which transactions and investments can be effected. Recognition would exempt exchanges from the need for authorisation as an investment business and provide a special regime for the scrutiny of competition. Membership of an exchange would not confer authorisation as an investment business and conduct of business rules would be introduced to provide comparable protection for transactions completed outside RIEs. The SIB was considering a number of candidates for RIE status, including: the Stock Exchange; the UK commodity and financial futures and options exchanges (37); a potential over the counter market exchange (38); and certain other overseas exchanges. No final decisions on SROs or RIEs could, however, be taken until after powers had been transferred to the Board. To obtain recognition an exchange would either have to establish its own internal clearing arrangements or use a recognised clearing house as an agent. Finally, it proposed that compensation schemes, to protect investors in cases where firms could not meet their obligations, should be established, since they are judged to be an essential part of investor protection (39).

Whilst the Bill was being drafted it became clear that the government had decided in favour of one regulatory board, rather than two. It announced in December 1985 that the SIB and Miboc would be merged into a single, hitherto unnamed, board. After consultations, in the period following the publication of the Bill until the end of the Parliamentary session in the Summer of 1986, the government made a series of changes to the Bill. The Board that will succeed the SIB is to have greater powers than envisaged in the Bill. Originally, once the Board had approved an SRO, it would only have been able to impose rule changes by agreement with the SRO or by taking it to court. This was because it was thought that practitioners would not shoulder the financial burden of running SROs unless they were given some autonomy. The SIB, however, successfully sought powers for the Board to impose its own rules on SROs or professional bodies in relation to their investment business. The regulatory structure took further shape in February and March 1986 when the SIB and Miboc published draft rules and sought comments. These incorporated the principle of independence, whereby investment advisors will be required to disclose their dealing interests to their clients. Further rules, issued by the SIB in May 1986, required money held on trust by authorised investment business to be kept in a separate client bank account. The aim is to protect the money in the event of a firm's insolvency. In the light of comments received, the SIB published revised draft rules in September 1986 which contained some substantial revisions. It became likely that the Board would in fact continue to be called the SIB and would receive powers in 1987, following the passing of the Financial Services Act. By August 1986 eighteen members of the SIB had been named by the DTI and the Bank. They included previous members of the SIB and Miboc, a number of lay members and some representatives of the City.

There have been a number of changes in the Bill resulting from pressure from backbench Conservative MPs in the committee stages of the legislation process. Backbench pressure led Mr Michael Howard, the Minister responsible for corporate and consumer affairs, to give an undertaking, in February 1986, that the SIB would have power to change the rule book of SROs without first obtaining a court order. This accorded with the wishes of the SIB, as mentioned above, and broadly satisfied Opposition MPs who continued to press for a stronger SIB with statutory commission status. In March 1986 the Opposition, with the help of Conservative representatives on the standing committee on the Bill, defeated the government and an amendment was passed naming the SIB and recognising it in law. This effectively forced the government to delegate powers to the SIB, unless it chose not to delegate after all. The change will have little effect, however, unless the government is persuaded to give the board adequate powers of investigation, enforcement and prosecution. The government was not willing to give such powers to a private sector regulator, which the SIB will remain despite the amendment. In May 1986 the government yielded further to pressure from backbench MPs. It accepted that the Trade and Industry Secretary could grant the SIB powers to prosecute, in certain circumstances, and that some investigatory powers could be delegated to the SIB.

In April 1986, members of the six nascent SROs appealed for legal immunity. They collectively decided that it would be impossible to invite members to join or to appoint officers unless SROs received a similar indemnity from litigation to that accorded to the SIB. This was because, if their actions were challenged in court by recalcitrant businesses, they would face potential bankruptcy because they would have few assets and they were unlikely to be able to insure against such unquantifiable losses. Without immunity the SROs would be inhibited in their dealings with larger investment business for fear of litigation. In May 1986 the government bowed to the pressures from the SROs and granted them immunity from being sued for negligence, either by their members or by the public. Paul Channon, the Trade and Industry Secretary, declared the move to be necessary on pragmatic grounds. Mr Channon also reacted to pressure from SROs by further modifying their relationship to the SIB. The latter would still be able to alter an SRO's rules, if it believed that they failed to provide adequate investor protection, but it would have to consult the SRO first and its decisions could be challenged in court. Further, if the SIB wished to change its own rules it would have to consult the SROs and other affected bodies first. The granting of legal immunity to the SROs was welcomed by the Chairman of the SIB.

Criticism of the Bill came from a number of quarters of the House of Commons during the Bill's four day committee stage in July 1986. The anxieties were reinforced by research commissioned by a major accountancy firm (40) which found that less than 20% of London's international securities and investment houses believed the Bill would provide a good regulatory framework. There was a risk that, following its consideration in the House of Lords, the Opposition peers would seek to reopen the committee stage in October 1986, rather than allow the legislation to move into its report stage as scheduled (41). This would have delayed the passing of the Act and might even have caused the government to lose the Bill through lack of Parliamentary time. The peers were unhappy about the large number of amendments tabled by the government for the Bill's final report stage. It is, however, perhaps not surprising that the international securities houses, which were to be regulated by Isro (42), have reservations about the Bill. It will introduce regulation to the Eurobond market, which they dominate, for the first time. They are concerned because the Bill is primarily concerned with protecting the private clients of investment businesses, rather than regulating the professional investment markets in which they deal. They had, however, been drawn into the overall regulatory structure when a different form of regulation might have been appropriate. Their response was to try to wring concessions out of the government and Isro successfully led the pressure group of SROs to secure legal immunity. They had a strong bargaining position because the government did not wish to drive Eurobond business overseas by over-regulation. They have also successfully persuaded the government to permit supporting bids to stabilise prices in the Eurobond market and are, with the backing of the Stock Exchange, also seeking permission to allow the practice, permitted in the US share markets, of price stabilisation in connection with new equity issues.

The prospects of the Bill were further complicated by a late submission, in August 1986, by the Association of Corporate Treasurers, which represents most large companies. It claimed that the Bill would cover many of the ordinary activities of non-financial companies and impose a heavy administrative burden on the SIB if hundreds of such companies had to be authorised. They argued that the Bill should be fundamentally restructured because it would create a 'regulatory minefield' for industrial and commercial companies. The government gave reassurances that the Bill would proceed to report stage in October 1986 and Mr Channon entered into discussions with the CBI (43) and the Association of Corporate Treasurers to establish which sections of the Bill required clarification so that changes could be introduced at the report stage.

Isro published its draft rules in September 1986 and later in the month the proposed merger between the Stock Exchange and Isro was announced, following lengthy consultations. If their members agreed, the Stock Exchange and Isro would be merged to form a new SRO called the Securities Association. This was welcomed by the SIB, since it would bring domestic and international securities trading under one organisation and reduce the number of proposed SROs, and by the Bank, since it would end the fragmentation of the international equity market. The merger was advocated by the Stock Exchange Council because the main objective of the reforms it had overseen had been to bring international equities trading within the Stock Exchange. Failure to sanction the merger, which would bring the major securities houses, with which many of the brokers and jobbers are now associated, within the new exchange, would probably mean that the Stock Exchange would witness a further loss of trade in the major international stocks. Apart from gaining direct entry to the Exchange, Isro's members would benefit by sharing the costs of establishing and staffing an SRO and from participating in the Stock Exchange's existing regulatory apparatus. In November 1986 the members of both the Stock Exchange and of Isro agreed to the merger. In addition the Stock Exchange members accepted: that membership could be extended to corporate entities, in addition to individuals as hitherto allowed; that unlimited liability of members would be ended, by converting the Stock Exchange into a limited company; and a compensation deal which, although an improvement on the deal rejected in 1985, was felt to be inadequate by many members. Opposers of the resolutions had hoped to negotiate better terms with Isro following their rejection. The fact that they were passed by substantial majorities, in excess of the 75% required, is a testament to Isro's bargaining power.

Although still to be called the Stock Exchange, its official title will be the International Stock Exchange in the UK and the Republic of Ireland and it will seek to become an RIE. The SRO will have a separate governing body from that of the RIE and the functions of authorisation and market operation, which the Stock Exchange had hitherto combined, will be separated. The SRO and the RIE will, however, have a single administration combining the Stock Exchange's existing one with Isro's small staff and additional staff with experience in international markets. The initial Council of the Exchange will consist of thirty-one people: fifteen appointed by the Stock Exchange and fifteen by Isro and a Chief Executive who will be a non-voting member. Representation on the governing body of the new SRO will also be equally divided (44). The RIE will not operate trading in Eurobonds but the Securities Association will authorise members to trade in the Eurobond market in London. The Swiss based Association of International Bond Dealers (AIBD), the trade association of approximately 800 firms trading in the Eurobond market which formed Isro, will apply to the SIB to be recognised as an RIE. The Securities Association's governing body and the AIBD Board are to form a permanent liaison committee to ensure effective co-operation. The merger agreement brought the major Japanese securities houses, which are prominent members of Isro, into the Stock Exchange without provision for reciprocal access of UK firms to the Tokyo exchange. This contravened government policy of pursuing reciprocity, which was itself written into the Bill, but, given the SIB's, the Bank's and the Stock Exchange's support for the merger, the goverment did not to oppose it.

Finally, in August 1986, in line with an EC directive on unit trusts and its responsibility for authorising and supervising them, the DTI published a consultative document on unit trusts. It proposed to allow trusts to undertake a wider range of business, subject to the discipline of enhanced disclosure, in line with the government's policy of promoting competition amongst investment institutions. Responsibility for authorisation is to be passed to the SIB, under clauses 73 and 77 of the Financial Services Bill, and changes will be made in the light of the European Council directive for collective investments in transferable securities (the Ucits directive), which aims to establish common rules for collective investments in securities within the EC.

The House of Commons finished considering and approved the 581 House of Lords amendments to the Financial Services Bill on the last day of October 1986 and it received royal assent at the end of the first week in November. It had taken 316 days to pass through Parliament. The SIB hoped to receive recognition as the designated agency by the end of 1986. The Office of Fair Trading will then have to check that its rules of conduct do not infringe competition law. This process was expected to be completed in the Spring of 1987 and the prospective SROs and RIEs would then be able to seek recognition from the SIB. If all went according to plan the new regulatory system would be in place in the Autumn of 1987 and investment businesses would then be required to seek authorisation. The compensation provisions were not finalised. These were left to the SIB to arrange. They seem likely to be more generous than originally proposed and a federal compensation scheme will probably be established, with individual SROs responsible for claims up to certain levels. Rules for complaints procedures and arrangements for the establishment of an Investment Ombudsman were also to be published at a future date. If the Big Bang causes major upheavals, then new legislation may have to be drafted, perhaps involving a statutory independent commission in line with the US Securities and Exchange Commission as favoured by the Opposition, before the currently envisaged legislation becomes fully operative. The time lag between the Big Bang and the implementation of the new regulatory structure proposed by the Bill could well prove to be unfortunate.

5.4 The Re-Regulation of the Building Societies

The 1986 Building Societies Act, which permits societies to broaden the scope of their activities within specified limits, transferred supervisory authority over the societies from the Chief Registrar of Friendly Societies to the Building Societies Commission (BSC). The BSC is to be given a wider range of powers than the Registrar had. It will be empowered to determine whether societies have exceeded the limits imposed on the deployment of assets and may order offenders to wind themselves up or to become companies. It will also be able to adjudicate on whether a society's proposals are within its powers. Hitherto such issues had been decided in open court. The Commission will also be given discretion to alter the provisions of the legislation through statutory instruments. It can, for example, permit societies to boost reserves by issuing subordinated loan stock.

The Act also detailed the provisions of a new government sponsored investor protection scheme, which broadly follows the banks' scheme. It is to be administered by a new Building Societies Investor Protection Board. If a society becomes insolvent, the Board may levy contributions from the other societies up to a maximum of 0.3% of the amount invested with it. Investors in insolvent societies will be paid up to 75% of their investments up to a compensation limit of £7,500. Societies will also be permitted, as previously, to enter into voluntary arrangements to provide more complete compensation and may also be allowed to lend to a society in difficulties. Also, in line with the Financial Services Bill and proposed bank supervisory legislation, there are proposals for an exchange of information between the regulators and the auditors.

The Chief Registrar of Friendly Societies, Mr Michael Bridgeman, was expected to become the First Commissioner of the BSC. The Registrar has for some time been concerned about the capital adequacy of building societies and the concern has increased in the light of the diversification in their activities to be permitted with effect from January 1987. From September 1986 the BSC, which will have more staff than the Registry, will have invested in it, as a body, many of the powers currently granted to the Registrar, as an individual. The Registrar published a consultative paper (45) on the capital adequacy of Societies in August 1986. It proposes a system to assess capital adequacy based on the Bank's banking supervision proposals (46). These would replace the eighteen year old system of prescribed reserves and are the culmination of four years' work by the Registry. Statutory minimum ratios would no longer be prescribed. Instead two measures of a society's capital requirements would be used: a measure intended to give the public a sense of the relative capital strengths of societies; and a group of operational measures. The public measure will be a ratio of free capital to total liabilities and no minimum will be set. The operational measure will not be published. It will be assessed by applying a set of formulae to the different types of activities undertaken. On top of these specific provisions it is proposed that there should be a general capital provision of 0.5% of total assets initially and that this should be increased to 1%, over a suggested five year period. Judgement of capital adequacy will take account of societies' subsidiaries through consolidated supervision, where appropriate. It was judged that societies satisfying the Commission on the operational measure would have acceptable public ratios.

The paper on capital adequacy also warned societies not to reduce liquidity much below the present generally accepted minimum norm of 15% of total assets. Societies hold their liquid funds primarily in the form of gilt-edged securities and/or local authority debts and it provides them with a cushion against big withdrawals by savers and allows them to meet peaks in mortgage demand. Demand for mortgages was buoyant in 1986 and mortgage lending provided a greater return than investment in securities. Societies, therefore, ran down their liquidity. In June it averaged 16.6%, the lowest since Spring 1984. It fell gain in July and the leading societies were aiming to reduce liquidity ratios to 15% by the year's end. In the 1980-85 period it averaged between 18.9% and 20.5%. A consultative paper on new liquidity regulations was due to be published in the Autumn of 1986, by the BSC.

The activities of the building societies and other mortgage lenders attracted attention from the Bank in September 1986. The Governor urged (47) them to show caution in their lending in the light of the growing incidence of mortgage arrears and repossessions, which grew by 54% in 1985. With the BSC supervising the building societies, the Bank most of the rest of the other mortgage lenders and the development of a secondary market a distinct possibility, it is to be hoped that the two authorities can ensure that there are no supervisory gaps, by co-operating closely. The fact that the proposed capital guidelines for societies follow closely those introduced by the Bank for banks is encouraging. A decision will have to be taken about who is to supervise the nascent secondary market though. Perhaps its main participants should be encouraged to establish an RIE in the future.

5.5 **Future Prospects**

Taken together, the regulatory and supervisory arrangements, for the banks, the building societies and the rest of the financial system, that are in place or being formulated, seem consistent. In order to make the supervisory system function smoothly and effectively it is essential that there is not an excessive number of supervisory authorities. The SIB is doing its best to ensure that there are not too many SROs and the merger of the Stock Exchange and Isro is an important step in this direction. It is essential to ensure that coverage is comprehensive, so that there are no regulatory and supervisory gaps. It is also essential to ensure that there is adequate co-operation between supervisory authorities, especially as the emerging financial conglomerates will be overseen by a number of authorities. The principle of lead supervision is important here. A key and contentious element of the new supervisory processes, the opening of a dialogue between supervisors and auditors, will hopefully be resolved satisfactorily in the near future. There are, however, a worrying number of loose ends which will not be tied up until well after the Big Bang. It would have been much more satisfactory to have the regulatory system operational before the major stock market reforms became effective.

The changes in regulatory structure discussed in this chapter amount to a major regulatory reform or re-regulation, rather than deregulation. The banking and building society sectors are to be more formally regulated and more strictly supervised, and regulatory and supervisory structures are to be put in place for the rest of the financial system - much of which was previously rather loosely supervised, by the DTI, and some of it, most importantly the Eurobond market, previously unsupervised.

Only time will tell whether the regulatory reform will be a success. The Big Bang is likely to bring casualties and there will probably be further incidences of fraud. The new system must be able to withstand these shocks. It must also adapt to further financial innovation and changes in the structure of the rapidly evolving and internationalising financial system. The system has built in flexibility and it must use it to ensure that the financial system is adequately supervised without encouraging business to move offshore to softer financial centres. Continued development of contacts with overseas supervisory authorities, to ensure international consistency, is thus essential. The general objective is to encourage efficiency through competition whilst protecting investors and depositors. To achieve this rules must exclude unsuitable businesses without creating new cartels to replace the old clublike arrangements that prevailed in the City. The supervisors must also ensure that adequate compensation funds are in place, so that inefficient firms can be allowed to fail and do not need to be bailed out by authorities. If the SROs are unable to afford to establish adequate funds individually, it will be more efficient to pool the various compensation funds and have the SIB oversee the pooled fund. This seems to be the most likely outcome despite the SEC's opposition. Care must also be taken to ensure that the legal immunity of the SROs does not encourage them to become lax in their supervision and responsive only to practitioners' interests, rather than to those of the investors they are supposed to protect. The appeals procedures must, therefore, be seen to be operating effectively. With regard to fraud, it is essential that auditors play a greater role in detection and that a more effective system of prosecuting its propagators be found. In the November 1986 Queen's Speech the government promised legislation, consistent with the Roskill Committee's Report (1986) on the prosecution of fraud, in the next Parliamentary session. Inaction might have caused investigators to become demoralised and the reputation of the City would have been difficult to restore. The use of new electronic technology has perhaps made fraud easier to perpetrate and increased its potential size. Security systems to prevent computer based fraud should be improved. Financial institutions have hitherto (48) been reticent about reporting such frauds, due to the potential impact on their public image and the small chance of successful prosecution.

One area causing some concern is the proposed reliance on 'Chinese Walls' separating the dealing, investment organising, and advisory departments of multipurpose financial institutions. For investor protection, it is essential that advice is not influenced by an institution's other interests. In some of the larger institutions, as many as fifty such walls could be needed and rigorous internal policing will be required. The practicality of this arrangement is debatable. An alternative would be to require a far greater amount of disclosure of a business's interests, to clients, than so far envisaged. Greater disclosure in general might also be helpful. It would reduce the need to place so much reliance on auditors in the detection of fraud and expose the institutions to greater market discipline.

More fundamentally, the decision to combine investor protection with comprehensive regulation of the financial system, including markets, such as the Eurobond market, dominated by professionals, is a matter of concern. Experience may well lead to different principles being applied, perhaps through SROs, for protecting private investors than those applied to professionals. As an alternative, different requirements could be imposed on the RIEs, in which professionals primarily deal, than on exchanges, such as the Stock Exchange, in which there is considerable public involvement. If the government wishes to encourage private share ownership it may find that further tax incentives are required, since commissions seem unlikely to fall appreciably for share trading in small amounts and may even rise, as was the case following the reform of the New York Stock Exchange in 1975. Otherwise, even the Stock Exchange will continue to move towards domination by institutional investors and professional dealers. This is especially likely following its merger with Isro.

If the Big Bang causes significant casualties, then the government may be forced, by public opinion, to introduce a more statutorily based supervisory system. With the SIB in place, this could be achieved by transforming it into a statutory body, vesting it with greater powers of investigation and enforcement and giving it the financial backing to perform its enhanced reponsibilities. A major crisis would be likely to lead to a formation of a government from the Opposition parties, which are committed to a more statutorily based supervisory structure. The Labour Party has promised, for example, that a future Labour government would introduce fresh legislation to regulate the City by 1989. The legislation would require greater disclosure, by compelling insurance companies to make their charges explicit to their customers for example. It would also introduce a statutory regulatory body with more independence from City interests than the SIB. There is a more widespread (49) concern that, by aiming to provide an all embracing regulatory framework for the financial system, the legislation has failed to concentrate primarily on consumers' interests. It has instead fallen between the two stools of investor protection and regulating markets dominated by professionals and has responded unduly to the latter's lobbying, aimed at protecting their own interests.

Notes

1. Commission of the European Communities (1977).

2. See Bank of England (1978), Channon (1977) and Reid (1982) for accounts of the crisis.

3. The UK Deposit Protection Fund became operational in February 1982 and met its first claim following the liquidation of an LDT in May 1982. LDTs and recognised banks were required to contribute to the fund in proportion to their deposit base and subject to maximum and minimum levels. In the event of insolvency depositors receive compensation from the fund equivalent to 75% of their 'protected deposits' and the maximum protected deposit for each depositor was set at £10,000. Building societies, Trustee Savings Banks, and the National Savings and Girobanks were exempt because they were judged to be satisfactorily regulated and supervised under statute.

4. See Bank of England (1980, 1981, 1982).

5. Which aims to co-ordinate the supervisory systems of the member countries of the EC. It was created in 1977 to assist the European Commission in implementing its banking directives.

6. The BIS is the central bankers' bank, see Hirsch (1969) for details of its origins and functions.

7. After its chairman, Mr W.P. Cooke of the Bank's Supervisory Division.

8. See Committee on Banking Regulations and Supervisory Practices (1975, 1983).

9. Taking account of not just a bank's accounts but also those of its domestic and foreign subsidiaries.

10. See Commission of the European Communities (1983a).

11. See Bank of England (1986b).

12. See note 4.

13. See Committee on Banking Regulations and Supervisory Practices (1986).

14. Bank for International Settlements (1986).

15. The ten major industrial countries that established the IMF's General Agreements to Borrow in 1961.

16. Command Paper 9432 (1985).

17. Which involved the rescue, in 1984, by the Bank of Johnson Matthey Bank (JMB), which was a subsidiary of the conglomerate Johnson Matthey Company, see Mullineux (1987, Appendix B). JMB was a recognised bank.

18. The Lloyd's Act.

19. It is based at the office of the Department of Public Prosecutions and co-ordinates efforts on major fraud investigations using lawyers and accountants from the Department of Trade and Industry. It works closely with the City Police Fraud Squad.

20. See Roskill Committee (1986).

21. Which erupted in 1982, see Lever and Huhne (1985).

22. The international loans were commonly made by

syndicates of banks, see Lever and Huhne (1985), since the loans required were often too large for individual banks.

23. See note 13.
24. See note 17.
25. Bank of England (1982a)
26. On 17 December 1984.
27. Command Paper 9550 (1985).
28. Command Paper 9695 (1985).
29. See Section 5.3.
30. See Gower Report (1984).
31. Command Paper 9432 (1985).
32. The National Association of Securities Dealers and Investment Managers, which appeared to be a model for the SRO requirements outlined in the White Paper.
33. Which deal directly, in equities and bonds, with their customers. The OTC market is separate from both the Eurobond market and the Stock Exchange and deals in international securities and UK unlisted securities. The Association of International Bond Dealers represents many of its participants, see below.
34. Insurance Brokers Registration Council.
35. House of Commons Bill 51.
36. "Regulation of Investment Business: The New Framework", Securities and Investment Board and Marketing of Investment Board Organising Committee.
37. Including the London International Financial Futures Exchange (Liffe), the London Metal Exchange (LME) and the London Commodity Exchange (LCE) .
38. To be run by the National Association of Securities Dealers and Investment Managers (Nasdim).
39. Sir Kenneth Berrill, Chairman of the SIB, discusses the proposed regulatory arrangements and the principles that have guided their determination further in the Midland Bank Review, Summer 1986, pp. 14-19.
40. Deloitte Haskins and Sells. The paper is entitled "Regulation and the Financial Services Bill, a City Research Associates Survey".
41. The report stage had originally been scheduled for June but had been postponed until October, due to congestion in the Lords.
42. The International Securities Regulatory Organisation.
43. Confederation of British Industry.
44. It is to have twenty-five members: a chairman who may be a practitioner; eighteen practitioners, nine appointed by the Stock Exchange Council (SEC) and nine by the Isro steering committee; and six lay members, three appointed by the SEC and three by Isro.
45. "Capital Adequacy. A Consultative Paper", Registry of Friendly Societies.
46. See Bank of England (1980).

47. At the World Congress of the International Union of Building Societies and Savings Associations, in Vienna, on 15 September 1986.

48. An exception was the case involving the London branch of Pru-Bache Securities, the US investment bank, in September 1986. The fraud involved an electronic transfer of Eurobond securities, worth $8.5 billion, and was detected at virtually the last minute. It involved unauthorised access to the computer system and was reported to the City of London Fraud Squad.

49. Shared by a number of consumers' organisations.

Chapter Six

UK BANKING AFTER DEREGULATION

In the 1970s the UK banking system changed considerably. The major clearing banks diversified their domestic retail and corporate business and became increasingly more international in their outlook as the Eurocurrency and syndicated loan markets grew apace. Merchant banks and discount houses also diversified and there was a resurgence of the commercial bill market and the introduction and growth of the certificates of deposit (1) market. Whilst the major clearers were developing their international business the building societies were rapidly expanding their branch networks and attracting a greater share of savings deposits, largely at the expense of the major clearing banks. Significant new competitors, such as the TSBs, the National Girobank and the Co-operative Bank, emerged as well. The clearers' diversification included the development, usually by acquisition, of finance house subsidiaries and also of merchant banking subsidiaries. As a result they could offer retail instalment credit and a greater array of services to the corporate sector, including leasing and factoring. Competition in the corporate banking sector, which the clearing banks had traditionally provided with working capital through overdraft facilities, was therefore heightened as the independent merchant banks also tried to maintain and expand their business. As the largely London based Euromarkets blossomed, there was an influx of foreign banks, adding to the competition. Additionally, the wholesale money markets grew rapidly, providing the banks with the opportunity of pursuing liability management and making them less reliant on their retail deposit base. Perhaps for this reason they were not unduly concerned about their loss of share in the savings market.

Although there was considerable diversification within the banking sector and some innovation, including the introduction of certificates of deposit and the re-emergence of commercial bills, traditional demarcations between the banking sector and the rest of the financial system, particularly its separation from the capital markets, remained largely intact. Following the removal of exchange controls in 1979, the rate of change accelerated. High inflation and unstable interest and exchange rates created an environment encouraging financial innovation. Technological innovations in the fields of communications and data processing allowed the freer flows of capital to respond increasingly to price movements. Money also flowed more freely following the removal of the 'corset' in 1980 and the subsequent removal of other restrictions on lending, such as term controls on consumer credit in 1982. The lifting of qualitative and quantitative credit controls eliminated rationing and increased the responsiveness of money flows to interest rates. Alongside the rise in inflation, these developments may have contributed to the rise in nominal interest rates in the early 1980s and probably explain the return to positive real interest rates which has been a feature of this period. Similar developments in the US have been interpreted in this way. Rising interest rates allow banks to widen the margins between lending and borrowing rates and also generate an endowment effect. This results because, commonly, no interest is paid on current account deposits so the margin on lending such deposits rises with the interest rate. The endowment effect is attenuated by the practice of not charging fully for money transmission services (MTS) provided through current accounts. With 'free banking' clearers waive all charges to customers except those with negative balances, who incur penal charges. Until 1985 the major clearers only waived charges for customers with specified positive balances, but charges to other customers did not fully recover the cost of providing the MTS. With automation the cost of providing MTS rose in the 1980s but not in line with the rise in interest rates. The banks therefore enjoyed benefits from the endowment effect and their profits rose significantly. The Chancellor responded, much to the chagrin of the banks, by imposing a windfall profits tax in the 1981 Budget. The banks pointed out that the endowment effect rose and fell with interest rates and at times was very small, if not negative, because of implicit interest paid to current account holders by virtue of the practice of not recovering the full costs of MTS through charges. They felt that a longer term view should have been taken by the Chancellor, especially as they were being urged by the Bank of England to build up their capital reserves and loan loss provisions.

Whilst nominal rates continued to fluctuate in the 1980s, expanding and contracting the endowment effect, real rates remained positive and even increased as the inflation rate fell faster than nominal interest rates. The banks' profits, therefore, remained healthy even though they continued to nurse a number of companies suffering from high interest rates and the effects of the recession in the early 1980s and to build up capital and to provision against their domestic and international, following the 1982 Mexican Crisis, loans. The endowment effect's contribution to profits will probably decline following the widespread adoption of free banking in 1985 and the fall in nominal interest rates in the mid 1980s. It could eventually be eliminated if the development of EFTPOS leads to full charging for MTS and if the practice of paying interest on current accounts becomes widespread as competition between banks and building societies increases. Whilst positive real interest rates remain it is hard to see how banks can fail to make sound profits unless these are impaired by bad management or problems amongst creditors.

The banks have benefited from the slow but sure economic recovery since 1982. This has been fuelled largely by consumer spending which has in turn been encouraged by falling inflation and rising real wages, despite the continued rise in unemployment and positive real interest rates. The fall in inflation has not only boosted real wages but also encouraged a rundown in savings balances. The persistent rise in consumer spending has had the additional benefit of creating a rapidly rising demand for consumer credit, which is traditionally a high margin and, therefore, profitable business. With growing opportunities in the domestic retail market and declining profitability in the international syndicated loan market, initially as a result of growing competition in the market and then as a result of the Mexican debt crisis and subsequent reschedulings for Third World debtors at finer margins, the major clearing banks switched emphasis in the first half of the 1980s. They attempted to recapture their share of the savings market: from the building societies, the increasingly competitive National Savings movement and the smaller clearing banks. They also began to diversify their retail services, by moving into the home loans market in particular. Meanwhile the building societies were continuing to develop their retail banking services, primarily by offering MTS. Demarcations between the savings institutions and the banks thus continued to be eroded. The tax reforms and legislation reforming the TSBs and the building societies, discussed in Chapter 4, are likely to reinforce this process and further increase competition.

The financial innovation that occurred in London's Euromarkets also had a major impact on the banking system. It opened a Pandora's box spawning two major developments: the blurring of distinctions between banks and non-bank financial intermediaries through securitisation; and the reduction of the potential of domestic monetary policy. In connection with the latter, interest rates have increased in importance as a channel for monetary policy because money has become more difficult both to define and to control. The usefulness of the practice of targeting money aggregates has thus been called into question (2). The relationship of money aggregates with policy goal variables, such as inflation, has been distorted by the tendency of money to be attracted to interest bearing financial assets (3) and by disintermediation (4). Only the very narrowest of aggregates, such as M0, is relatively free from such influences (5). In order to gauge the build up of liquidity, given the freedom of flows of funds between banks and building societies, it is necessary to monitor broader aggregates, such as PSL2. Sterling M3 has been the only consistently targeted aggregate during the early 1980s, but this has been distorted: by the removal of the 'corset' (6); by the increased proportion of money held in interest bearing accounts; and by flows of funds between savings institutions. Because of such distortions its target was abandoned in October 1985, although it was temporarily reinstated in the March 1986 Budget. These developments have forced the monetary authorities to adopt a more pragmatic approach to monetary control and place greater emphasis on exchange and interest rates. It seems likely that monetary aggregates will cease to be used as intermediate target variables and become one of a number of indicator variables instead. Financial innovations such as the development of a UK commercial paper market will add to the problem of interpreting movements in money aggregates (7), and so will further breakdowns in the traditional demarcations in the financial sector. As noted in Chapter 3, a fully deregulated electronic banking system would have little use for money as a physical medium of exchange and possibly only a numeraire would be required. In such a world there would be no need to control money aggregates. For further discussion of the implications of deregulation and financial innovation for monetary policy see: Bank for International Settlements (1986), Morris (1986), and Niehans (1983).

The securitisation process has led to a merging of the money and capital markets and encouraged a further erosion of the demarcations between financial institutions. The major clearing banks have become actively involved in the capital markets as a result. Having gained experience in the Eurobond markets, they have actively prepared for the Big Bang by building up investment banking groups which will allow them to make markets in equities and gilts. Many of the merchant banks also wish to take advantage of the new opportunities in the stock market and have metamorphosed into investment banks. The reform of the Stock Exchange combined with the government policy, backed by tax incentives, of encouraging wider share ownership provides the clearing banks with the opportunity of developing high street financial supermarkets offering a whole range of retail financial services. It seems likely, however, that specialists will remain in the retail and corporate markets and that they will earn a healthy income.

The UK financial system has traditionally been informally regulated and consequently there has not been much deregulation, in the literal sense, in the 1980s. Legislation has been passed to liberalise the building societies and privatise the TSBs and the Stock Exchange has agreed to remove its restrictive practices. The discount houses appear to be losing their privileged status and new markets, such as the commercial paper market, have been permitted to open. Also, lending controls have been lifted and taxes revised to remove distortions. Apart from this the picture has been one of re-regulation. The 1979 Banking Act introduced a more formal regulatory structure (8) and, following the Johnson Matthey Bank Affair, bank supervision has been tightened and the 1979 Act is to be amended accordingly (9). The building societies also face more formal regulation and supervision in accordance with the 1986 Building Societies Act and, after their privatisation in 1986, the TSBs are to be supervised by the Bank. Additionally, the government has introduced measures, which it intends to strengthen further, to improve the detection and successful prosecution of fraud and a supervisory system for the non-bank financial system. The latter is to be facilitated through self regulatory organisations (SROs) and recognised investment exchanges (RIEs), which will have to seek authorisation and approval of their rule books from the Securities and Investments Board (SIB). The SIB is to have powers delegated to it by the Department of Trade and Industry under the Financial Services Act (10). As a result, some sectors of the London financial markets, such as the Eurobond market, will be regulated and supervised for the first time and others will be more formally and directly supervised than before.

If inflation was the main driving force behind the financial innovation, then its decline to low levels, if sustained, should reduce the impetus for further innovations. In the absence of world monetary reform it is hard to see a reduction in exchange rate instability, unless international policy co-ordination is improved significantly. In order to counter exchange movements, interest rates, which are the only instruments able to respond quickly enough, will have to be used. Continued exchange and interest rate instability will ensure a healthy demand for hedging devices such as financial futures and options. Even if the pace of innovation slows in the latter half of the 1980s, the financial system is unlikely to revert to its previous form. Tricks once learnt are not easily forgotten and the innovation has probably improved the efficiency of the financial system by allowing it to satisfy more precisely the requirements of its users.

The prospects in the medium term depend on the post Big Bang scenario and the forthcoming general election (11). If the Big Bang is followed by a crisis the chances of a Labour victory will be increased. This is especially true in the light of the tarnished public image of the City following the high publicity given to the problems of Lloyd's (12), the Johnson Matthey Affair (13) and more widespread fraud in the City. In opposition, the Labour Party has committed itself to the introduction of fresh legislation to regulate the City by 1989. Labour aims to introduce an independent self standing statutory commission to police the City, in place of the SIB. Its wider plans for the City (14) have included the nationalisation of one or more of the major clearing banks and other financial institutions. These appear to have been dropped in favour of proposals to merge the National Savings Bank and the National Girobank, to create a People's Bank, and to form a National Investment Bank (NIB).

The formation of a People's Bank (15) is unlikely to stimulate a significant increase in competition for retail banking because it is already pretty intense and is likely to increase as a result of the privatisation of the TSBs and the reform of the building societies. The National Investment Bank would be modelled on similar institutions abroad (16). It is hoped that it would provide a systematic link between long term savings and real investment and overcome the failure of the financial system to supply long term funds for investment in industry. It would be jointly funded by pension funds, life assurance companies and the government. Initially the government would introduce tax incentives to encourage the repatriation of overseas portfolio investments held by UK institutions, which were built up rapidly following the lifting of exchange controls. In the longer term its lending might take the form of joint ventures with public and private sector banks and other financial institutions and it might consider extending its services to include loan guarantees to encourage commercial banks' participation. It would also consider the benefits of introducing a rediscounting facility to enable banks to transform their loans into more liquid assets and therefore to make them more willing to commit themselves to long term loans. The NIB would lend money on the basis of social, rather than purely pecuniary, returns and, where appropriate (17), at subsidised interest rates. The government would provide the interest rate subsidy, which would be separately accounted for.

It is proposed that the NIB should have a powerful regional dimension, working closely with, and providing funds for, local and regional planning agencies whose development Labour proposes to promote. The Labour Party feels that there is insufficient financial expertise within the existing public agencies concerned with industrial development and proposes to nationalise some institutions as part of the process of establishing the NIB. It is, therefore, possible that one or more merchant banks and insurance companies will be nationalised in this connection. Another candidate might be Investors in Industry (3i) (18), which is 85% owned by the major clearers and 15% owned by the Bank of England. There was speculation in 1985 that 3i was preparing to go public. Its business, which primarily involves extending venture capital, has increasingly overlapped with that of the major clearers and Midland Bank expressed a desire to sell its stake when it ran into trouble in 1985 (19). The astuteness of buying financial enterprises in the hope of acquiring expertise must, however, be questionable in the light of the experiences of firms acquiring or merging with jobbing and broking firms in the build up to the Big Bang. Having bought the firms, the acquirers often saw their staff enticed away by other institutions. Hence, nationalisation, which might anyway prove costly, should probably be kept to a minimum. It is far wiser, and clearly cheaper, to attract individuals with expertise by paying attractive salaries. Another motive for buying financial firms in preparation for the Big Bang was to build up contacts, but these too were often lost when individuals moved on. The need to acquire contacts in this way does not apply to the NIB because it is supposed to be filling a gap in the financial market where no contacts have previously existed.

The election of a Labour government could coincide with a trend towards re-regulation overseas. Sectors of the US banking system are still in a precarious position and the problems of the system as a whole could be compounded if the US growth continues to slow, as it threatens to do in 1987. This would weaken the corporate sector and might bring an end to the consumer boom (20). The system could be further buffeted by renewed problems amongst the Latin American debtors, whose export revenues would suffer if the slowdown in US growth were not offset by an increase in European and Japanese growth (21) and a trade war were to develop. In the mid 1980s protectionist and anti-banking sentiments were running high in the US. With the mid term Senate elections in 1986 delivering a Democratic Party majority and the Reagan administration's term coming to an end in 1988, the chances of successful protectionist and restrictive banking legislation being passed are increasing. A financial crisis would do little for Vice President George Bush's chances of election and would be likely to lead to a return of a less free market oriented administration.

There is growing concern that free capital flows, floating exchange rates and free trade are incompatible. Reform of the exchange rate system has so far been ruled out by the IMF and most of the

Group of Seven major industrial nations. President Reagan has, however, publicly requested the US Treasury to investigate and report on the merits of holding a conference on international monetary reform. If this initiative comes to nought and a trade war develops the long term effect may be to bring about international conferences to establish new world monetary and trading regimes, mirroring the post-war reaction to the experiences of the 1930s. Such developments might even lead to a reintroduction of restrictions on capital movements. This is unlikely and probably unnecessary, since it should be possible to establish a reformed international monetary system that can accommodate free capital flows. Its management would require a great deal of international co-operation, however. Hopefully, a trade war will not develop and the creeping protectionism that has been a feature of the 1980s will be reversed by the round of GATT negotiations announced in September 1986. It would be reprehensible for the world's leaders to sacrifice free trade for free capital flows whilst adopting a laissez-faire attitude towards the international monetary system.

In the more immediate future, and apart from the Big Bang, there is another possible cause of a financial crisis in the UK. As noted in Chapter 4, leading figures in the financial markets have warned about the growth in outstanding consumer credit. Their concern may be unwarranted because the credit growth has gone hand in hand with growing incomes and a rise in personal assets. The personal sector may, therefore, be able to support its debt. There has, however, been a growth in the number of houses repossessed by building societies and fuel and other debts are increasing with a resultant rise in County Court proceedings to recover debt. What seems to be happening is that borrowers with good credit ratings have arranged their financial affairs sensibly and, given the growing competition, more cheaply than in the past. The growth in competition has, however, led to an increase in lending to higher risk borrowers. This has been encouraged by the government's policy of expanding home ownership and the increased access to credit afforded by the lifting of credit controls and the spread of credit and charge cards. Should inflation and interest rates start to rise again and wage increases decline with falling corporate profitability, which might result if the UK economy remains sluggish after 1986, then credit will become more difficult to service.

The Bank of England is concerned that the build up in personal liquidity witnessed in the first half of the 1980s might eventually be reversed. This could result from a rise in inflation, caused initially by the depreciation of the pound that took place in 1986 and reinforced by wage inflation. Inflation had been reduced largely as a result of falling commodity prices but these were showing signs of recovery toward the end of 1986. A credit crisis would be exacerbated by a fall in the value of personal assets, particularly house prices. Although house prices have been rising rapidly in the South East in the first half of the 1980s, the rise elsewhere has been sluggish. Other countries, particularly the US but also Germany to a lesser extent, have experienced a period of falling house prices and land values in the 1980s. It is not impossible for the UK to experience a similar event, although it is more likely to occur outside the South East as the post oil boom house price slump in Aberdeen has shown.

Crisis apart, and even after the election of a centrist Labour government, the banking system is likely to enjoy a healthy and profitable future. The major banking groups are likely to become truly universal banks, offering a whole range of services to the retail and corporate sectors, and to be the dominant force in the post revolution financial system. The four major clearers may be joined by other universal banks, following a period of rationalisation amongst the smaller clearers, the building societies and other institutions such as merchant banks and perhaps the remaining independent discount houses. They will continue to compete, in the domestic and international banking markets, with the major European, Japanese and US banks and may even face competition at home from a public sector People's Bank. The NIB could well be established and may successfully fill a gap in the financial system. If the pace of innovation slackens, the regulators may eventually catch up and the banks will compete in an environment where continued international co-operation amongst the various domestic financial supervisory bodies has led to a fair amount of co-ordination in the supervision of international financial operations. Continued deregulation, broadly defined, is likely to go hand in hand with regulatory reform.

Notes

1. Which provide evidence of deposits made with banks and are repayable on a fixed date. Depositors can hold the certificates to maturity or sell them on the secondary market.

2. As enshrined in the "Medium Term Financial Strategy" which the government has pursued since 1980, see House of Commons (1980).

3. This can involve switches of money both between various components of an aggregate and more importantly between components of an aggregate and liquid assets excluded from the aggregate.

4. See Chapter 2.

5. Although the relatively slow growth of M0 could reflect the increased attractiveness of interest bearing assets.

6. See Chapter 2.

7. Since borrowing directly, using commercial paper, taps liquidity held by investment institutions and corporate treasurers without the intermediation of the banking system.

8. By introducing licensing requirements and extending the Bank of England's duties to include the supervision of secondary banks, thenceforth called licensed deposit takers, which had been previously rather loosely supervised by the Department of Trade and Industry.

9. See Chapter 5.

10. Which received royal assent in November 1986.

11. Scheduled for 1988, although the government is permitted to call an election at an earlier date if it wishes and there was speculation that the election would be called in the Summer or Autumn of 1987.

12. The London insurance underwriting market. It suffered from a number of cases involving fraud and malpractice in the early 1980s.

13. See Chapter 5.

14. See Labour Party Financial Institutions Study Group (1982).

15. Which was considered unnecessary by the Committee to Review the Functioning of Financial Institutions (1980), which could see no advantages, either through a significant increase in competition or from rationalisation, in the proposed merger.

16. Such as Credit National in France and the Japanese Development Bank.

17. For priority investment projects for example.

18. Previously Finance For Industry, which was formed in 1973 to act as a holding company for two institutions formed in 1945, at the request of the government, to fill a gap in financial provision for small and medium sized industrial firms.

19. Due to problems with Crocker Bank, its US subsidiary, which has subsequently been sold.

20. Which is anyway likely to be curtailed by budgetary reform, designed to reduce the US fiscal deficit, and tax reform, designed amongst other things, to reduce allowances on loans, which are extensive in the US, and to encourage savings.

21. This appears unlikely because both Germany and Japan have remained committed to fiscal austerity and had little room to reduce their interest rates significantly. Further the appreciation of their currencies has been reducing the competitiveness of their export sectors, which have traditionally led their growth.

REFERENCES

Bank for International Settlements (1985), Payment Systems in Eleven Developed Countries, Bank for International Settlements, February.

Bank for International Settlements (1986), Recent Innovations in International Banking, April, Basle, Switzerland.

Bank of England (1971) Competition and Credit Control, May, London.

Bank of England (1978), "The secondary banking crisis and the Bank of England's support operations", Bank of England Quarterly Bulletin, Vol. 18, No. 2, June, pp. 230-99.

Bank of England (1979), "Monetary base control", Bank of England Quarterly Bulletin, June, pp. 149-59.

Bank of England (1980), "The measurement of capital", Bank of England Quarterly Bulletin, September, pp. 324-9.

Bank of England (1981), "Foreign currency exposure", Bank of England Quarterly Bulletin, June, pp. 235-7.

Bank of England (1981a), "Developments in co-operation among bank supervisory authorities", Bank of England Quarterly Bulletin, June, pp.238-44.

Bank of England (1981b), 'Monetary Control Provisions', Bank of England, August.

Bank of England (1982a), "The measurement of liquidity", Bank of England Quarterly Bulletin, September, pp. 399-402.

Bank of England (1982b), "The role of the bank supervisor", Bank of England Quarterly Bulletin, December, pp. 547-52.

References

Bank of England (1982c), "The supplementary special deposit scheme", Bank of England Quarterly Bulletin, March, pp. 74-85.

Bank of England (1985a), The Future Structure of the Gilt-Edged Market: The Bank of England's Dealing and Supervisory Relationships with Certain Participants, April.

Bank of England (1985b), Report and Accounts.

Bank of England (1985c) "Services in the UK economy", Bank of England Quarterly Bulletin, September, pp. 404-14.

Bank of England (1986a), "Innovations in International Banking, Governor's Speech", Bank of England Quarterly Bulletin, June, pp. 225-9.

Bank of England (1986b) "Consolidated supervision of institutions authorised under the Banking Act 1979", Bank of England Quarterly Bulletin, March, pp. 85-9.

The Banker (1986), EFTPOS: Slow Progress, February, pp. 75-84.

Black, F. (1970), "Banking and interest rates in a world without money", Journal of Bank Research, Autumn, pp. 9-20.

Brown, R. (1982), A Guide to Monetary Policy, Bank Information Service, London.

Channon, D.F. (1977), British Banking Strategy, Macmillan, London.

Coghlan, R. (1980), The Theory of Money and Finance, Macmillan, London.

Command Paper 3292 (1967), 'Bank Charges', National Board for Prices and Incomes, HMSO.

Command Paper 7858 (1980), Monetary Control, HMSO, March.

Command Paper 9125 (1984), 'Review of Investor Protection', Dept. of Trade and Industry, Part 1, Report, L.C.B. Gower, HMSO.

Command Paper 9316 (1984), Building Societies: A New Framework, HMSO, July.

Command Paper 9415 (1984), Trustee Savings Banks, HMSO.

Command Paper 9432 (1985), Financial Services in the UK: A New Framework for Investor Protection, HMSO, June.

Command Paper 9550 (1985), Report of the Committee Set Up to Consider the System of Banking Supervision, HMSO, July.

Command Paper 9695 (1985), Banking Supervision, HMSO, December.

Commission of the European Communities (1977), First Council Directive, OJ, No. L332, 17 December.

Commission of the European Communities (1983a), Council Directive of 13 June on the Supervision of Credit Institutions on a Consolidated Basis, (83/350/EEC), Brussels.

Commission of the European Communities (1983b), Financial Integration, COME(83) 207 Final, 20 April, Brussels.

Commission of the European Communities (1985), Steps to European Unity, 5th Edition, EC.

Commission of the European Communities (1986), Programme for the Liberalisation of Capital Movements in the Community, Com(86), 292.

Committee of London Clearing Bankers (CLCB) (1978), The London Clearing Banks, Longman, London.

Committee of London Clearing Bankers (CLCB) (1979), The Bank Nationalisation Debate 1975-1978, London.

Committee on Banking Regulations and Supervisory Practices (1975), The Basle Concordat, December, Basle, Switzerland. See also "Developments in co-operation among bank supervisory authorities", Bank of England Quarterly Bulletin, June, 1981.

Committee on Banking Regulations and Supervisory Practices (1978), Consolidation of Banks' Balance Sheets: Aggregation of Risk Bearing Assets as a Method of Supervising Bank Solvency, October, Basle, Switzerland.

Committee on Banking Regulations and Supervisory Practices (1983), Principles for the Supervision of Banks' Foreign Establishments, May, Basle, Switzerland.

Committee on Banking Regulations and Supervisory Practices (1986), The Management of Banks Off Balance Sheet Exposures: A Supervisory Perspective, March, Basle, Switzerland.

Committee to Review the Functioning of Financial Institutions (Wilson Committee) (1979), Interim Report on the Financing of Small Firms, March, Cmnd 7503.

Committee to Review the Functioning of Financial Institutions

References

(Wilson Committee) (1980), Report and Appendices, HMSO, Cmnd 7937.

Congdon, T. (1981), "The first principles of central banking", The Banker, April, pp. 57-62.

Cooper, J. (1984), "The management and regulation of banks", Chapter 5, The Prudential Supervision of Banks, Macmillan, London.

Dennis, G. and Nellis, J. (1984), "The EMS and UK membership: five years on", Lloyds Bank Review, No. 154, October, pp. 13-31.

Dunham, C.R. and Syron, R.F. (1984), "Interstate banking - part II", New England Bank Review, May/June, pp. 11-28.

European Commission (1985), see Commission of the European Communities (1985).

European Commission (1986), see Commission of the European Communities (1986).

European Communities (1983a, b), see Commission of the European Communities (1983a, b).

Fama, E.F. (1980), "Banking in the theory of finance", Journal of Monetary Economics, Vol. 6, pp. 39-57.

Germany, D. and Morton, J. (1985), "Financial innovations and deregulation in foreign industrial countries", Federal Reserve Bulletin, October, pp. 743-53.

Gower Report (1984) - see Command Paper 9125.

Goode, R.M. (1985), Electronic Banking: The Legal Implications, Institute of Bankers.

Grubel, H.G. (1984), The International Monetary System, 4th Edn, Penguin, Harmondsworth, Middlesex.

Haney, S. (1985), "An example to the West", The Banker, November, pp. 34-6.

Heaton, G.G. and Dunham, C.R. (1985), "The growing competitiveness of credit unions", New England Economic Review, May/June, pp. 29-34: Federal Reserve Bank of Boston.

Hirsch, F. (1969), 'Money International', Penguin Books, Harmondsworth, Middlesex.

Hirsch, F. (1977), "The Bagehot problem", The Manchester School, pp. 241-57.

House of Commons (Red Book) (1980), Financial Statement and Budget Report 1980/81, HMSO.

House of Commons (1985a), Financial Services Bill, HC238, 1985/86.

House of Commons (1985b), Building Society Bill, HC95, 1985/86.

Inter-Bank Research Organisation (IBRO) (1982), IBRO Research Brief, October.

Kraft, J. (1984), The Mexican Rescue, Group of Thirty, New York.

Labour Party (1973), Banking and Insurance Green Paper, Report of a Labour Party Study Group, London.

Labour Party (1979), Final Report of the Working Party on Banking and Insurance, London.

Labour Party Financial Institutions Study Group (1982), The City: A Socialist Approach, The Labour Party, London.

Lever, H. and Huhne, C. (1985), Debt and Danger, Penguin Books, Harmondsworth, Middlesex.

Macmillan (1931), Report of the Committee on Finance and Industry, (Macmillan Report), Cmnd 3897.

Members of the Bankers Clearing House (1984), Payment Clearing Systems: Review of Organisation, Membership and Control, (Child Report), December.

Midland Bank (1984), "Economic outlook", Midland Bank Review, Autumn, pp. 2-4.

Monopolies Commission (1968), Barclays Bank Ltd, Lloyds Bank Ltd, and Martins Bank: A Report on the Proposed Merger, HMSO.

Morris, F.E. (1986), "The changing world of central banking", New England Economic Review, pp. 3-6: Federal Reserve Bank of Boston.

Mullineux, A.W. (1987) UK Banking After Deregulation, Croom Helm, London.

National Consumer Council (1983), Banking Services and the Consumer: A Report by the National Consumer Council, Methuen.

References

National Executive Committee (1976), Banking and finance, The Labour Party, London.

Niehans, J. (1978), The Theory of Money, John Hopkins University Press, Baltimore and London.

Niehans, J. (1983), "Financial innovation, multinational banking and monetary policy", Journal of Banking and Finance, 7, pp. 537-51.

Pecchioli, R.M. (1983), The Internationalisation of Banking: The Policy Issues, OECD, Paris.

Price Commission (1978), Banks: Charges for Money Transmission Services, HMSO, April.

Reid, M. (1982), The Secondary Banking Crisis: 1973-1975, Macmillan, London.

Revell, J. (1975), "Solvency and regulation of banks", Bangor Occasional Paper in Economics No. 5, University of Wales Press.

Roskill Committee (1986) 'Report', Fraud Trials Committee, E.W. Roskill, January, HMSO.

Rybcynski, T.M. (1985), "Financial systems, risk and public policy", Royal Bank of Scotland Review, No. 148, December, pp. 35-45.

Simpson, T.D. and Parkinson, P.M. (1984), "Some implications of financial innovations in the United States", Staff Studies 139, Board of Governors of the Federal Reserve System, Washington DC.

Syron, R.F. (1984), "The New England experiment in interstate banking", New England Bank Review, March/April, pp. 5-17.

Terry, N.G. (1985), "The 'Big Bang' at the Stock Exchange", Lloyds Bank Review, No. 156, April, pp. 16-30.

Tobin, J. (1963), "Commercial banks as creators of credit", in Carlson, D. (ed.), Banking and Monetary Studies, Irwin, Homewood, Illinois.

White, B. and Vittas, D. (1986), "Barriers in international banking", Lloyds Bank Review, No. 161, July, pp. 19-31.

INDEX